MW00535278

FAVORITE SECRET RESTAURANT RECIPES

pil

Publications International, Ltd.

Copyright © 2024 Publications International, Ltd.
All rights reserved. This publication may not be reproduced or quoted in whole or in part by any means whatsoever without written permission from:

Louis Weber, CEO
Publications International, Ltd.
8140 Lehigh Ave
Morton Grove, IL 60053

Permission is never granted for commercial purposes.

Pictured on the front cover (*clockwise from top left*): Crazy Breadsticks (*page 21*), Southwestern Chicken Chili (*page 52*), Strawberry Cream Shortcake (*page 160*), Barbecue Chicken Pizza (*page 114*), Wedge Salad (*page 80*) and Lemon Ricotta Pancakes (*page 10*).

Pictured on the back cover (*left to right*): Pumpkin Spice Latte (*page 18*), Double Decker Tacos (*page 96*) and Red Velvet Cookies (*page 174*).

ISBN: 978-1-63938-551-5

Manufactured in China.

8 7 6 5 4 3 2 1

Microwave Cooking: Microwave ovens vary in wattage. Use the cooking times as guidelines and check for doneness before adding more time.

Note: This book was not licensed or endorsed by and is not affiliated with or approved by any of the owners of the trademarks or brand names referred to in the book.

WARNING: Food preparation, baking and cooking involve inherent dangers: misuse of electric products, sharp electric tools, boiling water, hot stoves, allergic reactions, foodborne illnesses and the like, pose numerous potential risks. Publications International, Ltd. (PIL) assumes no responsibility or liability for any damages you may experience as a result of following recipes, instructions, tips or advice in this publication.

While we hope this publication helps you find new ways to eat delicious foods, you may not always achieve the results desired due to variations in ingredients, cooking temperatures, typos, errors, omissions or individual cooking abilities.

Let's get social!
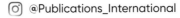
@Publications_International
@PublicationsInternational
www.pilbooks.com

TABLE OF CONTENTS

BREAKFAST AND BRUNCH

INSPIRED BY STARBUCKS®

BLUEBERRY MUFFINS
MAKES 12 MUFFINS

2 cups all-purpose flour

2¼ teaspoons baking powder

½ teaspoon salt

¼ teaspoon baking soda

1 cup granulated sugar

½ cup (1 stick) butter, melted

¾ cup buttermilk

2 eggs

1 teaspoon grated lemon peel

1½ cups blueberries

2 tablespoons sparkling sugar *or*
4 tablespoons turbinado sugar

1 Preheat oven to 375°F. Line 12 standard (2½-inch) muffin cups with paper baking cups or spray with nonstick cooking spray.

2 Combine flour, baking powder, salt and baking soda in medium bowl; mix well. Whisk granulated sugar and butter in large bowl until well blended. Add buttermilk, eggs and lemon peel; whisk until well blended. Add flour; stir just until dry ingredients are moistened. Gently fold in blueberries.

3 Divide batter evenly between prepared muffin cups (cups will be almost full). Sprinkle ½ teaspoon sparkling sugar or 1 teaspoon turbinado sugar over each muffin.

4 Bake 20 to 22 minutes or until toothpick inserted into centers comes out clean. Cool in pan 10 minutes; remove to wire rack. Serve warm or cool completely.

CLASSIC BREAKFAST SANDWICH
MAKES 2 SERVINGS

2 English muffins, split
2 tablespoons butter, divided
2 slices American cheese

2 slices Canadian bacon
2 eggs
½ cup water

1 Toast English muffins; spread cut sides with 1 tablespoon butter. Place one slice cheese on each bottom muffin half.

2 Melt ½ tablespoon butter in medium nonstick skillet over medium heat. Add Canadian bacon; cook about 2 minutes per side or until lightly browned. Remove to plate.

3 Spray insides of two round metal biscuit cutters (2⅞ to 3¼ inches) or quart-size canning rings with nonstick cooking spray. Melt remaining ½ tablespoon butter in same skillet over medium heat. Place rings in skillet; crack one egg into each ring and break yolk with fork. Pour water into skillet around rings; cover and cook 2 to 3 minutes or until eggs are set.

4 Gently remove eggs from rings. Place on cheese-topped muffin halves; top with Canadian bacon and remaining muffin halves. Wrap each sandwich in foil; let stand 2 minutes before serving. (Steam will melt cheese and blend flavors.)

PUMPKIN DONUT MINIS
MAKES 36 DOUGHNUTS

½ cup granulated sugar

4 teaspoons ground cinnamon, divided

2 cups all-purpose flour

½ cup packed brown sugar

1½ teaspoons baking powder

½ teaspoon salt

½ teaspoon ground ginger

½ teaspoon ground nutmeg

¼ teaspoon baking soda

2 eggs

½ cup canned pumpkin

¼ cup (½ stick) butter, softened

¼ cup milk

1 teaspoon vanilla

¼ cup (½ stick) butter, melted

1 Preheat oven to 350°F. Spray 36 mini (1¾-inch) muffin cups with nonstick cooking spray. Combine granulated sugar and 3 teaspoons cinnamon in shallow dish; set aside.

2 Combine flour, brown sugar, baking powder, remaining 1 teaspoon cinnamon, salt, ginger, nutmeg and baking soda in medium bowl; mix well. Beat eggs, pumpkin, softened butter, milk and vanilla in large bowl with electric mixer at medium speed until well blended. Gradually add flour mixture; beat just until blended. Spoon scant tablespoonful batter into each prepared muffin cup.

3 Bake 12 minutes or until toothpick inserted into centers comes out clean. Cool in pans 2 minutes.

4 Working with one donut at a time, brush all over with melted butter and roll in cinnamon-sugar to coat. Return to wire racks to cool slightly. Serve warm or cool completely.

LEMON RICOTTA PANCAKES
MAKES 4 SERVINGS

1½ cups all-purpose flour
¼ cup granulated sugar
1 teaspoon baking powder
1 teaspoon baking soda
1 teaspoon salt
1½ cups ricotta cheese
1 cup buttermilk
2 eggs

½ cup lemon juice, divided
3 to 4 tablespoons vegetable oil, divided
2 tablespoons grated lemon peel, plus additional for garnish
1 cup powdered sugar
Fresh berries
Maple syrup

1 Combine flour, granulated sugar, baking powder, baking soda and salt in large bowl; mix well. Whisk ricotta, buttermilk, eggs, ¼ cup lemon juice, 2 tablespoons oil and 2 tablespoons lemon peel in medium bowl until well blended. Add to flour mixture; stir just until combined. Let batter stand 5 minutes.

2 Heat 1 tablespoon oil in large skillet over medium heat or brush griddle with oil. For each pancake, drop ⅓ cup batter into skillet, spreading into 5-inch circle. Cook 2 to 3 minutes or until bottom is golden brown and small bubbles appear on surface. Turn pancake; cook 2 minutes or until golden brown. Add additional oil to skillet as needed. To keep pancakes warm while cooking in batches, remove pancakes to wire rack set in baking sheet and place in 200°F oven.

3 Whisk remaining ¼ cup lemon juice into powdered sugar in small bowl until smooth. For each serving, stack three pancakes; drizzle with lemon glaze and top with berries. Garnish with additional lemon peel; serve with maple syrup.

BACON GRUYÈRE EGG BITES

MAKES 12 EGG BITES

6 eggs
1 cup cottage cheese
¾ cup (3 ounces) grated Gruyère cheese
¼ cup (1 ounce) grated Monterey Jack cheese

¼ teaspoon white vinegar
¼ teaspoon hot pepper sauce
Pinch salt and black pepper
6 slices bacon, cooked and crumbled

1 Preheat oven to 300°F. Generously spray 12 standard (2¼-inch) muffin cups with nonstick cooking spray.

2 Combine eggs, cottage cheese, Gruyère, Monterey Jack, vinegar, hot pepper sauce, salt and pepper in blender or food processor; blend until smooth.

3 Pour egg mixture evenly into prepared muffin cups; top with bacon (scant 1 tablespoon per cup). Press bacon lightly into egg mixture.

4 Bake 25 to 27 minutes or until set and toothpick inserted into centers comes out with a few moist crumbs. (Egg bites will puff up during baking and sink while cooling.) Cool in pan on wire rack 5 minutes. Loosen edges with small knife or spatula; remove to plate. Serve warm or at room temperature.

STRAWBERRY BANANA FRENCH TOAST
MAKES 2 SERVINGS

1 cup sliced fresh strawberries (about 8 medium)

2 teaspoons granulated sugar

2 eggs

½ cup milk

3 tablespoons all-purpose flour

1 teaspoon vanilla

⅛ teaspoon salt

1 tablespoon butter

4 slices (1 inch thick) egg bread or country bread

1 banana, cut into ¼-inch slices

Whipped cream and powdered sugar (optional)

Maple syrup

1 Combine strawberries and granulated sugar in small bowl; toss to coat. Set aside while preparing French toast.

2 Whisk eggs, milk, flour, vanilla and salt in shallow bowl or pie plate until well blended. Melt ½ tablespoon butter in large skillet over medium-high heat. Working with two slices at a time, dip bread into egg mixture, turning to coat completely; let excess drip off. Add to skillet; cook 3 to 4 minutes per side or until golden brown. Repeat with remaining butter and bread slices.

3 Top each serving with strawberry mixture and banana slices. Garnish with whipped cream and powdered sugar; serve with maple syrup.

FRITTATA RUSTICA
MAKES 2 SERVINGS

4 ounces cremini mushrooms, stems trimmed, cut into thirds

1 tablespoon olive oil, divided

½ teaspoon plus ⅛ teaspoon salt, divided

½ cup chopped onion

1 cup packed chopped stemmed lacinato kale

½ cup halved grape tomatoes

4 eggs

½ teaspoon Italian seasoning

Black pepper

⅓ cup shredded mozzarella cheese

1 tablespoon shredded Parmesan cheese

Chopped fresh parsley (optional)

1 Preheat oven to 400°F. Spread mushrooms on small baking sheet; drizzle with 1 teaspoon oil and sprinkle with ⅛ teaspoon salt. Roast 15 to 20 minutes or until well browned and tender.

2 Heat remaining 2 teaspoons oil in small (6- to 8-inch) ovenproof nonstick skillet over medium heat. Add onion; cook and stir 5 minutes or until soft. Add kale and ¼ teaspoon salt; cook 10 minutes or until kale is tender, stirring frequently. Add tomatoes; cook and stir 3 minutes or until tomatoes are soft. Stir in mushrooms.

3 Preheat broiler. Whisk eggs, remaining ¼ teaspoon salt, Italian seasoning and pepper in small bowl until well blended.

4 Pour egg mixture over vegetables in skillet; stir gently to mix. Cook 3 minutes or until eggs are set around edge, lifting edge to allow uncooked portion to flow underneath. Sprinkle with mozzarella and Parmesan.

5 Broil 3 minutes or until eggs are set and cheese is browned. Cut evenly into four wedges. Garnish with parsley.

PUMPKIN SPICE LATTE
MAKES 2 SERVINGS

1¾ cups milk, divided
½ cup canned pumpkin
3 tablespoons packed brown sugar
1 teaspoon grated fresh ginger
1 teaspoon pumpkin pie spice
½ teaspoon ground cinnamon, plus additional for garnish
¼ teaspoon salt

⅛ teaspoon coarsely ground black pepper
1 cup strong-brewed hot coffee*
1 tablespoon vanilla
Whipped cream (optional)

Use about 1 tablespoon ground espresso roast or other dark roast coffee for each 3 ounces of water.

1 Combine ½ cup milk, pumpkin, brown sugar, ginger, pumpkin pie spice, ½ teaspoon cinnamon, salt and pepper in medium saucepan; whisk until well blended. Cook over medium-low heat 10 minutes, whisking frequently. Remove from heat; whisk in coffee and vanilla. Strain through fine-mesh strainer into medium bowl.

2 Bring remaining 1¼ cups milk to a simmer in small saucepan over medium-high heat. For froth, whisk vigorously 30 seconds. Whisk into coffee mixture until blended. Garnish with whipped cream and additional cinnamon.

COFFEE FRAPPUCCINO
MAKES 1 (16-OUNCE) SERVING

½ cup ground coffee (preferably dark roast)
1 cup water
½ cup milk
¼ cup sweetened condensed milk

2 tablespoons vanilla instant pudding and pie filling mix
1 tablespoon maple syrup
1 cup ice cubes (about 6 cubes)
Whipped cream and unsweetened cocoa powder (optional)

1 Brew strong coffee using ground coffee and water.* (You should get about ½ cup coffee.) Refrigerate until cold.

2 Combine ¼ cup coffee, milk, sweetened condensed milk, pudding mix, maple syrup and ice in blender; blend until smooth. Garnish with whipped cream and cocoa.

This drink requires very strong coffee. If you don't have a coffee maker, you can use 2 tablespoons instant coffee blended with 2 tablespoons hot water or just enough water to dissolve the coffee. Proceed with step 2 as directed.

PUMPKIN SPICE LATTE

APPETIZERS

INSPIRED BY LITTLE CAESARS®

CRAZY BREADSTICKS
MAKES 16 BREADSTICKS

¼ cup (½ stick) butter, melted

¾ teaspoon garlic salt

1 container (about 14 ounces) refrigerated pizza dough

¼ cup grated Parmesan cheese

Pizza sauce or marinara sauce (optional)

1 Preheat oven to 425°F. Line baking sheet with parchment paper. Combine butter and garlic salt in small bowl; mix well.

2 Unroll dough on prepared baking sheet. Cut crosswise into 16 strips; spread strips out slightly on baking sheet so they are not touching. Brush with butter mixture.

3 Bake about 8 minutes or until golden brown. Immediately sprinkle with cheese. Serve warm with pizza sauce, if desired.

ZESTY LEMON-PEPPER WINGS
MAKES 8 SERVINGS

2 pounds chicken wings, tips discarded, separated at joints

⅔ cup all-purpose flour

1 teaspoon garlic powder

1 teaspoon onion powder

¾ teaspoon salt

½ teaspoon paprika

½ teaspoon black pepper

Vegetable oil for frying

¼ cup (½ stick) butter, melted

2 tablespoons lemon-pepper seasoning

1 teaspoon dried parsley

Ranch dressing or favorite dipping sauce (optional)

Lemon wedges and vegetable sticks (optional)

1 Place wings in large resealable food storage bag. Combine flour, garlic powder, onion powder, salt, paprika and pepper in small bowl; mix well. Add to bag with chicken: seal bag and toss to coat.

2 Heat 3 inches of oil in large saucepan or Dutch oven over medium-high heat to 350°F; adjust heat to maintain temperature. Set wire rack over paper towels.

3 Add wings to hot oil; cook 10 minutes or until crisp and browned and chicken is cooked through. Drain on prepared wire rack.

4 Meanwhile, combine melted butter, lemon-pepper and parsley in large bowl; mix well. Add wings; toss well to coat. Serve immediately with ranch dressing, lemon wedges and vegetables, if desired.

JALAPEÑO FETA DIP

MAKES ABOUT 1 CUP

1 jalapeño pepper, halved, stemmed and seeded

½ red onion, halved and separated

3 tablespoons plus 1 teaspoon olive oil, divided

8 ounces feta cheese

1 tablespoon water

1 Preheat oven to 400°F. Place jalapeño and onion on small baking sheet; drizzle with 1 teaspoon oil and stir to coat. Arrange vegetables cut sides down on baking sheet.

2 Roast 20 minutes or until vegetables are softened and slightly charred around edges. Let stand until cool enough to handle.

3 Scrape skin from jalapeño with paring knife. Coarsely chop jalapeño and onion.

4 Combine feta, remaining 3 tablespoons oil and water in food processor; process until smooth and fluffy. Add vegetables; pulse 6 to 8 times or until blended but still chunky. Store in airtight container in refrigerator up to 1 week.

TIP

Serve this dip with a sliced baguette, pita bread wedges, pita chips and/or cut-up fresh vegetables. Or you can use it as a spread on toast, sandwiches and wraps.

BUFFALO CAULIFLOWER BITES
MAKES 8 SERVINGS

¾ cup all-purpose flour
¼ cup cornstarch
1 teaspoon salt
½ teaspoon garlic powder
¼ teaspoon black pepper
1 cup water

1 large head cauliflower
   (2½ pounds), cut into
   1-inch florets
½ cup hot pepper sauce
¼ cup (½ stick) butter, melted
   Blue cheese or ranch dressing
   and celery sticks

1 Preheat oven to 450°F. Line baking sheet with foil; spray foil with nonstick cooking spray.

2 Whisk flour, cornstarch, salt, garlic powder and black pepper in large bowl. Whisk in water until smooth and well blended. Add cauliflower to batter in batches; stir to coat. Arrange on prepared baking sheet.

3 Bake 20 minutes or until cauliflower is lightly browned.

4 Meanwhile, combine hot pepper sauce and butter in small bowl; mix well. Pour over hot cauliflower; toss to coat. Bake 5 to 10 minutes or until cauliflower is glazed and crisp, stirring occasionally. Serve with blue cheese dressing and celery sticks.

CHICKEN LETTUCE WRAPS

MAKES 6 TO 8 SERVINGS

1 tablespoon vegetable oil

1 small onion, finely chopped

5 ounces cremini mushrooms, finely chopped (about 2 cups)

1 pound ground chicken

¼ cup hoisin sauce

2 tablespoons soy sauce

1 tablespoon rice vinegar

1 tablespoon sriracha sauce

1 tablespoon oyster sauce

2 cloves garlic, minced

1 teaspoon grated fresh ginger

1 teaspoon dark sesame oil

½ cup finely chopped water chestnuts

2 green onions, thinly sliced

1 head butter lettuce

1 Heat vegetable oil in large skillet over medium-high heat. Add onion; cook and stir 2 minutes. Add mushrooms; cook 8 minutes or until lightly browned and liquid has evaporated, stirring occasionally.

2 Add chicken; cook 8 minutes or until no longer pink, stirring to break up meat. Stir in hoisin sauce, soy sauce, vinegar, sriracha, oyster sauce, garlic, ginger and sesame oil; cook 4 minutes. Add water chestnuts; cook and stir 2 minutes or until heated through. Remove from heat; stir in green onions.

3 Separate lettuce leaves. Spoon about ¼ cup chicken mixture into each lettuce leaf. Serve immediately.

SPINACH AND FETA STUFFED CHEESY BREAD

MAKES ABOUT 8 SERVINGS

1½ cups (6 ounces) shredded mozzarella or Monterey Jack cheese, divided

4 ounces crumbled feta cheese

¼ cup plus 1 tablespoon grated Parmesan cheese, divided

1 teaspoon minced garlic

1 container (11 ounces) refrigerated French bread dough

1 cup baby spinach

½ cup (2 ounces) shredded Cheddar cheese

¼ teaspoon Italian seasoning or dried parsley flakes

1 Preheat oven to 350°F. Line baking sheet with parchment paper.

2 Combine 1 cup mozzarella, feta, ¼ cup Parmesan and garlic in small bowl; mix well.

3 Unroll dough on prepared baking sheet with long side facing you. Spread half of cheese mixture lengthwise over half of dough; top with spinach and remaining half of cheese mixture. Fold dough in half over filling; press long edge gently to seal.

4 Cut crosswise into 1-inch slices (but do not separate slices). Top with Cheddar, then with remaining ½ cup mozzarella. Sprinkle with Italian seasoning.

5 Bake 25 to 30 minutes or until golden brown. Serve warm.

CORN SALSA

MAKES ABOUT 2½ CUPS

1 large poblano pepper

1 package (16 ounces) frozen yellow or white corn

¼ cup diced red onion

¼ cup chopped fresh cilantro

1 large jalapeño pepper, seeded and finely chopped

1 tablespoon lime juice

1 tablespoon lemon juice

½ teaspoon salt

⅛ teaspoon black pepper

1 Preheat oven to 400°F. Line small baking pan with foil.

2 Roast poblano pepper on prepared pan about 40 minutes or until skin is charred and blistered, turning occasionally.

3 Remove pepper to small bowl; cover with plastic wrap and let stand 10 minutes to loosen skin. Peel and dice poblano pepper, discarding stem and seeds.

4 Meanwhile, cook corn according to package directions; cool to room temperature in refrigerator or freezer.

5 Place corn in large bowl. Add poblano, onion, cilantro, jalapeño, lime juice, lemon juice, salt and pepper; mix well. Let stand at least 30 minutes to blend flavors.

CRISPY PICKLE CHIPS
MAKES 4 TO 6 SERVINGS

4 large whole dill pickles
½ cup all-purpose flour
¼ teaspoon salt
⅛ teaspoon black pepper
1 egg

1 cup panko bread crumbs
2 tablespoons grated Parmesan cheese
Ranch dressing or garlic mayonnaise

1 Preheat oven to 450°F. Line baking sheet with parchment paper.

2 Cut pickles diagonally into ¼-inch slices. Pat dry with paper towels, removing as much excess moisture as possible.

3 Combine flour, salt and pepper in shallow dish. Beat egg in another shallow dish. Combine panko and cheese in third shallow dish. Dip pickle slices first in flour, then in egg, letting excess drip back into dish. Roll in panko mixture to coat, pressing lightly to adhere. Place in single layer on prepared baking sheet.

4 Bake 8 minutes or until bottoms are golden brown. Turn and bake 6 to 8 minutes or until golden brown and crisp. Serve warm with ranch dressing.

TEX-MEX NACHOS

MAKES 4 TO 6 SERVINGS

8 ounces ground beef

½ cup chopped onion

2 cloves garlic, minced

2 teaspoons chili powder

1 teaspoon ground cumin

½ teaspoon salt

½ teaspoon dried oregano

1 can (about 15 ounces) kidney beans, rinsed and drained

½ cup corn

½ cup sour cream, divided

2 tablespoons mayonnaise

1 tablespoon lime juice

¼ to ½ teaspoon chipotle chili powder

½ bag tortilla chips

½ (15-ounce) jar Cheddar cheese dip, warmed

½ cup pico de gallo

¼ cup guacamole

1 cup shredded iceberg lettuce

2 jalapeño peppers, thinly sliced into rings

1 Combine beef, onion and garlic in large skillet; cook and stir over medium-high heat 6 to 8 minutes or until beef is no longer pink, stirring to break up meat.

2 Add chili powder, cumin, salt and oregano; cook and stir 1 minute. Stir in beans and corn. Reduce heat to medium-low; cook 3 minutes or until heated through.

3 Combine ¼ cup sour cream, mayonnaise, lime juice and chipotle chili powder in small bowl; mix well. Pour chipotle sauce into small plastic squeeze bottle.

4 Spread tortilla chips on platter or large plate. Top with beef mixture; drizzle with cheese dip. Top with pico de gallo, guacamole, remaining ¼ cup sour cream, lettuce and jalapeños. Squeeze chipotle sauce over nachos. Serve immediately.

CHICKEN BACON QUESADILLAS

MAKES 4 SERVINGS

4 teaspoons vegetable oil, divided

4 (8-inch) flour tortillas

1 cup (4 ounces) shredded Colby-Jack cheese

2 cups coarsely chopped cooked chicken

4 slices bacon, crisp-cooked and coarsely chopped

½ cup pico de gallo, plus additional for serving

Sour cream and guacamole (optional)

1 Heat large nonstick skillet over medium heat; brush with 1 teaspoon oil. Place one tortilla in skillet; sprinkle with ¼ cup cheese. Spread ½ cup chicken over one half of tortilla; top with one fourth of bacon and 2 tablespoons pico de gallo.

2 Cook 1 to 2 minutes or until cheese is melted and bottom of tortilla is lightly browned. Fold tortilla over filling, pressing with spatula.

3 Remove to cutting board; cool slightly. Cut into wedges. Repeat with remaining ingredients. Serve with additional pico de gallo, sour cream and guacamole, if desired.

POTATO SKINS

MAKES 8 SERVINGS

8 medium baking potatoes (6 to 8 ounces each), unpeeled

1 tablespoon vegetable oil

1 teaspoon salt

⅛ teaspoon black pepper

1 tablespoon butter, melted

1 cup (4 ounces) shredded Cheddar cheese

8 slices bacon, crisp-cooked and coarsely chopped

1 cup sour cream

3 tablespoons snipped fresh chives

1 Preheat oven to 400°F.

2 Prick potatoes all over with fork. Rub oil over potatoes; sprinkle with salt and pepper. Place in 13×9-inch baking pan. Bake 1 hour or until fork-tender. Let stand until cool enough to handle. *Reduce oven temperature to 350°F.*

3 Cut potatoes in half lengthwise; cut small slice off bottom of each half so potato halves lay flat. Scoop out soft centers of potato skins; reserve for another use. Return potato halves, skin sides up, to baking pan; brush potato skins with butter.

4 Bake 20 to 25 minutes or until crisp. Turn potatoes over; top with cheese and bacon. Bake 5 minutes or until cheese is melted. Cool slightly. Top with sour cream and chives just before serving.

ONION RING STACK

MAKES 4 TO 6 SERVINGS (ABOUT 20 ONION RINGS)

1 cup all-purpose flour, divided

½ cup cornmeal

1 teaspoon black pepper

½ teaspoon salt, plus additional for seasoning

¼ to ½ teaspoon ground red pepper

1 cup light-colored beer

Rémoulade Sauce (recipe follows) or ranch dressing

Vegetable oil for frying

6 tablespoons cornstarch, divided

2 large sweet onions, cut into ½-inch rings and separated

1 Combine ½ cup flour, cornmeal, black pepper, ½ teaspoon salt and red pepper in large bowl; mix well. Whisk in beer until well blended. Let batter stand 1 hour.

2 Prepare Rémoulade Sauce; refrigerate until ready to serve.

3 Heat 2 inches of oil in large saucepan or Dutch oven over medium-high heat to 360° to 370°F; adjust heat to maintain temperature. Line large wire rack with paper towels.

4 Whisk 4 tablespoons cornstarch into batter. Combine remaining ½ cup flour and 2 tablespoons cornstarch in medium bowl. Thoroughly coat onions with flour mixture.

5 Working with one at a time, dip onion rings into batter to coat completely; carefully place in hot oil. Cook about four onion rings at a time 3 minutes or until golden brown, turning once. Remove to prepared wire rack; season with additional salt. Return oil to 370°F between batches. Serve immediately with Rémoulade Sauce.

RÉMOULADE SAUCE

Combine 1 cup mayonnaise, 2 tablespoons coarse-grain mustard, 1 tablespoon lemon juice, 1 tablespoon sweet relish, 1 teaspoon horseradish sauce, 1 teaspoon Worcestershire sauce and ¼ teaspoon hot pepper sauce in medium bowl; mix well.

SPINACH-ARTICHOKE DIP
MAKES 6 TO 8 SERVINGS

1 package (8 ounces)
   baby spinach

1 package (8 ounces) cream
   cheese, softened

¼ cup mayonnaise

1 clove garlic, minced

1 teaspoon dried basil

½ teaspoon dried thyme

¼ teaspoon salt

¼ teaspoon red pepper flakes

¼ teaspoon black pepper

1 can (about 14 ounces)
   artichoke hearts,
   drained and chopped

¾ cup grated Parmesan cheese,
   divided

Toasted French bread slices
   or tortilla chips

1 Preheat oven to 350°F. Spray 8-inch oval, round or square baking dish with nonstick cooking spray.

2 Place spinach in large microwavable bowl; cover and microwave on HIGH 2 minutes or until wilted. Uncover; let stand until cool enough to handle. Squeeze dry and coarsely chop.

3 Whisk cream cheese, mayonnaise, garlic, basil, thyme, salt, red pepper flakes and black pepper in medium bowl until well blended. Stir in spinach, artichokes and ½ cup Parmesan. Spread in prepared baking dish; sprinkle with remaining ¼ cup Parmesan.

4 Bake about 30 minutes or until edges are golden brown. Cool slightly; serve warm with bread.

SOUPS

INSPIRED BY PANERA BREAD®

BROCCOLI CHEESE SOUP
MAKES 4 TO 6 SERVINGS

6 tablespoons (¾ stick) butter
1 cup chopped onion
1 clove garlic, minced
¼ cup all-purpose flour
2 cups vegetable broth
2 cups milk
1½ teaspoons Dijon mustard
½ teaspoon salt
¼ teaspoon ground nutmeg

¼ teaspoon black pepper
⅛ teaspoon hot pepper sauce
1 package (16 ounces) frozen broccoli (5 cups)
2 carrots, shredded (1 cup)
6 ounces pasteurized process cheese product, cubed
1 cup (4 ounces) shredded sharp Cheddar cheese, plus additional for garnish

1 Melt butter in large saucepan or Dutch oven over medium-low heat. Add onion; cook and stir 8 minutes or until softened. Add garlic; cook and stir 1 minute. Increase heat to medium. Whisk in flour until smooth; cook and stir 3 minutes without browning.

2 Gradually whisk in broth and milk. Add mustard, salt, nutmeg, black pepper and hot pepper sauce; cook 15 minutes or until thickened, stirring occasionally.

3 Add broccoli; cook 15 minutes. Add carrots; cook 10 minutes or until vegetables are tender.

4 Remove half of soup to food processor or blender; process until smooth. Return to saucepan. Add cheese product and 1 cup Cheddar; cook and stir over low heat until cheese is melted. Garnish soup with additional Cheddar.

ROTISSERIE CHICKEN NOODLE SOUP
MAKE ABOUT 8 SERVINGS

½ (9-ounce) package no-boil
   lasagna noodles*
1 tablespoon olive oil or butter
2 large carrots, chopped
2 stalks celery, chopped
1 small onion, chopped
1 clove garlic, minced
½ teaspoon dried thyme
½ teaspoon dried oregano
¼ teaspoon dried basil
8 cups chicken broth

1 teaspoon salt
½ teaspoon black pepper
1 bay leaf
2 cups shredded rotisserie
   chicken
2 tablespoons finely chopped
   fresh parsley

*Or substitute 4 to 6 ounces
uncooked egg noodles and omit
step 1. Add uncooked noodles to
soup as directed in step 5.*

1 Spread lasagna noodles in 13×9-inch baking dish or other shallow pan;
cover with hot water. Let soak 10 minutes to soften, moving noodles
around occasionally to prevent sticking to each other.

2 Meanwhile, heat oil in large saucepan or Dutch oven over medium heat.
Add carrots, celery and onion; cook about 8 minutes or until vegetables
are softened, stirring occasionally.

3 Add garlic, thyme, oregano and basil; cook and stir 2 minutes. Stir in
broth, salt, pepper and bay leaf; bring to a boil over high heat.

4 Drain noodles, cut into 3×¾-inch strips. (Cut noodles crosswise into
¾-inch-wide strips, then cut each strip in half.)

5 Add noodles and chicken to broth mixture; return to a boil. Cook over
medium heat about 10 minutes or until noodles are tender, stirring
frequently. Remove bay leaf; stir in parsley.

ITALIAN WEDDING SOUP

MAKES 8 SERVINGS

MEATBALLS

- 2 eggs
- 2 cloves garlic, minced
- 1 teaspoon salt
- ⅛ teaspoon black pepper
- 1½ pounds meat loaf mix (ground beef and pork)
- ¾ cup plain dry bread crumbs
- ½ cup grated Parmesan cheese
- 2 tablespoons olive oil

SOUP

- 1 onion, chopped
- 2 carrots, chopped
- 4 cloves garlic, minced
- 2 heads escarole or curly endive, coarsely chopped
- 8 cups chicken broth
- 1 can (about 14 ounces) Italian plum tomatoes, undrained, coarsely chopped
- 3 sprigs fresh thyme
- 1 teaspoon salt
- ½ teaspoon red pepper flakes
- 1 cup uncooked acini di pepe pasta

1 For meatballs, whisk eggs, 2 cloves garlic, 1 teaspoon salt and black pepper in large bowl until blended. Stir in meat loaf mix, bread crumbs and cheese; mix gently until well blended. Shape mixture by tablespoonfuls into 1-inch balls.

2 Heat oil in large saucepan or Dutch oven over medium heat. Cook meatballs in batches 5 minutes or until browned. Remove to plate; set aside.

3 For soup, add onion, carrots and 4 cloves garlic to saucepan; cook and stir 5 minutes or until onion is lightly browned. Add escarole; cook and stir 2 minutes or until wilted. Stir in broth, tomatoes with juice, thyme, 1 teaspoon salt and red pepper flakes; bring to a boil over high heat. Reduce heat to medium-low; cook 15 minutes.

4 Add meatballs and pasta to soup; return to a boil over high heat. Reduce heat to medium; cook 10 minutes or until pasta is tender. Remove and discard thyme sprigs before serving.

SOUTHWESTERN CHICKEN CHILI

MAKES 6 SERVINGS

1 tablespoon vegetable oil

1 small onion, chopped

1 small red bell pepper, diced (¼-inch pieces)

1 jalapeño pepper, finely chopped

6 cloves garlic, minced

3 tablespoons all-purpose flour

2 tablespoons chili powder

1 tablespoon ground cumin

2 teaspoons salt

1 can (about 15 ounces) kidney beans, rinsed and drained

1 can (about 14 ounces) chicken broth

1 can (8 ounces) tomato sauce

1 can (4 ounces) diced green chiles

2 tablespoons chopped fresh cilantro

3 cups shredded cooked chicken

Optional toppings: shredded Cheddar cheese, chopped red onion, blue corn tortilla chips

1 Heat oil in large saucepan over medium heat. Add onion; cook about 5 minutes or until translucent, stirring occasionally. Add bell pepper, jalapeño and garlic; cook and stir 3 minutes.

2 Add flour, chili powder, cumin and salt; cook and stir 1 minute or until spices are fragrant.

3 Stir in beans, broth, tomato sauce, chiles and cilantro; bring to a boil. Reduce heat to low; cover and simmer 20 minutes, stirring occasionally.

4 Stir in chicken; cover and simmer 20 minutes. If chili is too thin, cook, uncovered, until slightly thickened. Serve with desired toppings.

BEEF VEGETABLE SOUP

MAKES 6 TO 8 SERVINGS

1½ pounds cubed beef stew meat

¼ cup all-purpose flour

3 tablespoons vegetable oil, divided

1 onion, chopped

2 stalks celery, chopped

3 tablespoons tomato paste

2 teaspoons salt

1 teaspoon dried thyme

½ teaspoon garlic powder

¼ teaspoon black pepper

6 cups beef broth, divided

1 can (28 ounces) stewed tomatoes, undrained

1 tablespoon Worcestershire sauce

1 bay leaf

4 unpeeled red potatoes (about 1 pound), cut into 1-inch pieces

3 medium carrots, cut in half lengthwise and cut into ½-inch slices

6 ounces green beans, trimmed and cut into 1-inch pieces

1 cup frozen corn

1 Combine beef and flour in medium bowl; toss to coat. Heat 1 tablespoon oil in large saucepan or Dutch oven over medium-high heat. Cook beef in two batches 5 minutes or until browned, adding additional 1 tablespoon oil after first batch. Remove to medium bowl.

2 Heat remaining 1 tablespoon oil in same saucepan. Add onion and celery; cook and stir 5 minutes or until softened. Add tomato paste, salt, thyme, garlic powder and pepper; cook and stir 1 minute.

3 Stir in 1 cup broth, scraping up browned bits from bottom of saucepan. Stir in remaining 5 cups broth, tomatoes with juice, Worcestershire sauce, bay leaf and beef; bring to a boil.

4 Reduce heat to low; cover and simmer 1 hour and 20 minutes. Add potatoes and carrots; cook 15 minutes. Add green beans and corn; cook 15 minutes or until vegetables are tender. Remove and discard bay leaf before serving.

CREAMY TOMATO SOUP

MAKES 6 SERVINGS

3 tablespoons olive oil, divided

2 tablespoons butter

1 large onion, finely chopped

2 cloves garlic, minced

2 teaspoons sugar

1 teaspoon salt

½ teaspoon dried oregano

2 cans (28 ounces each) peeled Italian plum tomatoes, undrained

4 cups ½-inch focaccia cubes (half of 9-ounce loaf)

½ teaspoon freshly ground black pepper

½ cup whipping cream

1 Heat 2 tablespoons oil and butter in large saucepan or Dutch oven over medium-high heat. Add onion; cook and stir 5 minutes or until softened.

2 Add garlic, sugar, salt and oregano; cook and stir 30 seconds. Stir in tomatoes with juice; bring to a boil. Reduce heat to medium-low; simmer 45 minutes, stirring occasionally.

3 Meanwhile, prepare croutons. Preheat oven to 350°F. Combine focaccia cubes, remaining 1 tablespoon oil and pepper in large bowl; toss to coat. Spread on large rimmed baking sheet. Bake 10 minutes or until bread cubes are golden brown.

4 Blend soup with hand-held immersion blender until smooth. (Or process soup in batches in food processor or blender.) Stir in cream; cook until heated through. Serve soup topped with croutons.

PASTA FAGIOLI

MAKES 8 SERVINGS

2 tablespoons olive oil, divided
1 pound ground beef
1 cup chopped onion
1 cup diced carrots
   (about 2 medium)
1 cup diced celery
   (about 2 stalks)
3 cloves garlic, minced
4 cups beef broth
1 can (28 ounces) diced
   tomatoes
1 can (15 ounces) tomato sauce
1 tablespoon cider vinegar

2 teaspoons sugar
1½ teaspoons dried basil
1¼ teaspoons salt
1 teaspoon dried oregano
¾ teaspoon dried thyme
2 cups uncooked ditalini pasta
1 can (about 15 ounces) dark
   red kidney beans, rinsed
   and drained
1 can (about 15 ounces)
   cannellini beans, rinsed
   and drained
Grated Romano cheese

1 Heat 1 tablespoon oil in large saucepan or Dutch oven over medium-high heat. Add beef; cook 5 minutes or until browned, stirring to break up meat. Remove to medium bowl with slotted spoon. Drain fat.

2 Heat remaining 1 tablespoon oil in same saucepan over medium-high heat. Add onion, carrots and celery; cook and stir 5 minutes or until vegetables are tender. Add garlic; cook and stir 1 minute.

3 Stir in cooked beef, broth, tomatoes, tomato sauce, vinegar, sugar, basil, salt, oregano and thyme; bring to a boil. Reduce heat to medium-low; cover and simmer 30 minutes.

4 Add pasta and beans; cook over medium heat 10 minutes or until pasta is tender, stirring frequently. Sprinkle with cheese.

HARVEST PUMPKIN SOUP
MAKES 8 SERVINGS

1 sugar pumpkin or acorn
   squash (about 2 pounds)
1 kabocha or butternut squash
   (about 2 pounds)
   Salt and black pepper
2 tablespoons olive oil
2 tablespoons butter
1 large onion, finely chopped
2 stalks celery, chopped
1 medium carrot, chopped
¼ cup packed brown sugar
2 tablespoons tomato paste

1 tablespoon minced
   fresh ginger
1 clove garlic, minced
1 teaspoon salt
1 teaspoon ground cinnamon
¼ teaspoon ground cumin
¼ teaspoon black pepper
4 cups vegetable broth
1 cup milk
2 teaspoons lemon juice
   Roasted pumpkin seeds
   (optional, see Tip)

1 Preheat oven to 400°F. Line large baking sheet with foil; spray with nonstick cooking spray.

2 Cut pumpkin and kabocha squash in half; remove and discard seeds and strings or reserve seeds to roast (see Tip). Season cut sides with salt and pepper. Place cut sides down on prepared baking sheet; bake 30 to 45 minutes or until fork-tender. When squash is cool enough to handle, remove skin; chop flesh into 1-inch pieces.

3 Heat oil and butter in large saucepan or Dutch oven over medium-high heat. Add onion, celery and carrot; cook and stir 5 minutes or until vegetables are tender. Add brown sugar, tomato paste, ginger, garlic, 1 teaspoon salt, cinnamon, cumin and ¼ teaspoon pepper; cook and stir 1 minute. Stir in broth and squash; bring to a boil. Reduce heat to medium; cook 20 minutes or until squash is very soft.

4 Blend soup with hand-held immersion blender until desired consistency. (Or process in batches in food processor or blender.) Stir in milk and lemon juice; cook until heated through. Garnish with pumpkin seeds.

TIP

Roasted pumpkin seeds can be found at many supermarkets, or you can roast the seeds that you remove from the pumpkin (and the squash) in the recipe. Combine the seeds with 1 teaspoon vegetable oil and ⅛ teaspoon salt in a small bowl; toss to coat. Spread in a single layer on a small foil-lined baking sheet; bake at 300°F 20 to 25 minutes or until the seeds begin to brown, stirring once.

HEARTY TUSCAN SOUP
MAKES 6 TO 8 SERVINGS

1 teaspoon olive oil

1 pound bulk mild or hot Italian sausage*

1 medium onion, chopped

3 cloves garlic, minced

¼ cup all-purpose flour

5 cups chicken broth

1 teaspoon salt

½ teaspoon Italian seasoning

3 medium unpeeled russet potatoes (about 1 pound), halved lengthwise and thinly sliced

2 cups packed torn stemmed kale leaves

1 cup half-and-half or whipping cream

Or use sausage links and remove from casings.

1 Heat oil in large saucepan or Dutch oven over medium-high heat. Add sausage; cook 5 minutes or until sausage begins to brown, stirring to break up meat.

2 Add onion and garlic; cook about 5 minutes or until onion is softened and sausage is browned, stirring occasionally.

3 Stir in flour until blended. Add broth, salt and Italian seasoning; bring to a boil.

4 Stir in potatoes and kale. Reduce heat to medium-low; cook 15 to 20 minutes or until potatoes are fork-tender. Reduce heat to low; stir in half-and-half. Cook about 5 minutes or until heated through.

CHICKEN ENCHILADA SOUP

MAKES 8 TO 10 SERVINGS

2 tablespoons vegetable oil, divided

1½ pounds boneless skinless chicken breasts, cut into ½-inch pieces

½ cup chopped onion

2 cloves garlic, minced

2 cans (about 14 ounces each) chicken broth

3 cups water, divided

1 cup masa harina

1 package (16 ounces) pasteurized process cheese product, cubed

1 can (10 ounces) mild red enchilada sauce

1 teaspoon chili powder

½ teaspoon salt

½ teaspoon ground cumin

1 large tomato, seeded and chopped

Crispy tortilla strips*

If tortilla strips are not available, crumble tortilla chips into bite-size pieces.

1 Heat 1 tablespoon oil in large saucepan or Dutch oven over medium-high heat. Add chicken; cook and stir 10 minutes or until no longer pink. Transfer to medium bowl with slotted spoon; drain any excess liquid from saucepan.

2 Heat remaining 1 tablespoon oil in same saucepan over medium-high heat. Add onion and garlic; cook and stir 3 minutes or until softened. Stir in broth.

3 Whisk 2 cups water into masa harina in large bowl until smooth. Whisk mixture into broth in saucepan. Stir in remaining 1 cup water, cheese product, enchilada sauce, chili powder, salt and cumin; bring to a boil over high heat.

4 Stir in chicken. Reduce heat to medium-low; cook 30 minutes, stirring frequently. Serve soup topped with tomato and tortilla strips.

SALADS

INSPIRED BY SEASONS 52® FRESH GRILL

TOMATO WATERMELON SALAD
MAKES 4 SERVINGS

DRESSING

¼ cup extra virgin olive oil

2 tablespoons lemon juice

½ teaspoon honey

½ teaspoon salt

⅛ teaspoon black pepper

SALAD

2 large heirloom tomatoes (about 10 ounces each), cut into 6 slices each

2 cups cubed watermelon (about 12 ounces)

¼ cup thinly sliced red onion rings

¼ cup crumbled feta cheese

Chopped fresh chervil or parsley (optional)

1 For dressing, whisk oil, lemon juice, honey, salt and pepper in small bowl until well blended.

2 For salad, arrange tomato slices on four plates. Top with watermelon and onion; sprinkle with cheese. Drizzle with dressing; garnish with chervil.

PROTEIN POWER SALAD
MAKES 4 SERVINGS

ROASTED TOMATOES
- 6 plum tomatoes, halved and seeded
- 2 tablespoons olive oil
- 1 tablespoon balsamic vinegar
- Salt and black pepper

DRESSING
- ¼ cup balsamic vinegar
- 2 tablespoons honey
- 1 tablespoon Dijon or whole grain mustard
- ½ teaspoon salt
- ¼ teaspoon black pepper
- ½ cup olive oil

SALAD
- 4 cups baby kale
- 4 cups arugula or spinach
- 1 pouch (about 8 ounces) precooked mixed grains,* prepared according to package directions
- 1 cup drained canned chickpeas
- 1 cup diced cucumber
- 4 hard-cooked eggs, peeled and chopped

Look for a mix of quinoa, barley, millet, flax, brown rice and wild rice.

1 For roasted tomatoes, preheat oven to 450°F. Line large baking sheet with foil.

2 Arrange tomatoes cut sides up on prepared baking sheet. Drizzle with 2 tablespoons oil and 1 tablespoon vinegar; season lightly with salt and pepper. Roast about 30 minutes or until tomatoes are very soft and slightly charred in spots. Coarsely chop when cool enough to handle.

3 Meanwhile for dressing, whisk ¼ cup vinegar, honey, mustard, ½ teaspoon salt and ¼ teaspoon pepper in medium bowl. Slowly whisk in ½ cup oil in thin, steady stream until well blended.

4 For each salad, combine 1 cup kale and 1 cup arugula in individual serving bowl; top with ½ cup grains and ¼ cup chickpeas. Arrange ¼ cup cucumber, one egg and one fourth of tomatoes on greens around grains. Drizzle 2 to 3 tablespoons dressing over each salad.

AMAZING APPLE SALAD

MAKES 4 SERVINGS (1 CUP DRESSING)

DRESSING

- 5 tablespoons apple juice concentrate
- ¼ cup white balsamic vinegar
- 1 tablespoon lemon juice
- 1 tablespoon sugar
- 1 clove garlic, minced
- ½ teaspoon salt
- ½ teaspoon onion powder
- ¼ teaspoon ground ginger
- ¼ cup extra virgin olive oil

SALAD

- 12 cups mixed greens such as chopped romaine lettuce and spring greens
- 12 ounces thinly sliced cooked chicken
- 2 tomatoes, cut into wedges
- 1 package (about 3 ounces) dried apple chips
- ½ red onion, thinly sliced
- ½ cup crumbled gorgonzola or blue cheese
- ½ cup pecans, toasted*

To toast pecans, cook in small skillet over medium-low heat 4 to 5 minutes or until lightly browned, stirring frequently.

1 For dressing, whisk apple juice concentrate, vinegar, lemon juice, sugar, garlic, salt, onion powder and ginger in small bowl until blended. Slowly whisk in oil in thin, steady stream until well blended.

2 For salad, divide greens among four serving bowls. Top with chicken, tomatoes, apple chips, onion, cheese and pecans.

3 Drizzle about 2 tablespoons dressing over each salad.

CRUNCHY KALE SALAD
MAKES 6 SERVINGS

¼ cup cider vinegar
¼ cup extra virgin olive oil
¼ cup maple syrup
1 tablespoon lemon juice
½ tablespoon Dijon mustard
½ teaspoon salt
¼ teaspoon black pepper

10 cups chopped stemmed kale (about 1 large bunch)
2 cups shredded green cabbage
½ cup sliced almonds, toasted*

To toast almonds, cook in small skillet over medium-low heat 2 to 3 minutes or until fragrant, stirring frequently.

1 Whisk vinegar, oil, maple syrup, lemon juice, mustard, salt and pepper in small bowl or measuring cup until well blended.

2 Combine kale and cabbage in large bowl. Pour dressing over vegetables; massage kale with hands 3 to 4 minutes to soften.

3 Stir in almonds just before serving.

SPINACH SALAD
MAKES 4 SERVINGS

DRESSING
- ¼ cup balsamic vinegar
- 1 clove garlic, minced
- ½ teaspoon sugar
- ¼ teaspoon salt
- ⅛ teaspoon black pepper
- ¼ cup olive oil
- ¼ cup vegetable oil

SALAD
- 8 cups packed baby spinach
- 1 cup diced tomatoes (about 2 medium)
- 1 cup drained mandarin oranges
- 1 cup glazed pecans*

- ½ cup crumbled feta cheese
- ½ cup diced red onion
- ½ cup dried cranberries
- 1 can (3 ounces) crispy rice noodles**
- 4 teaspoons toasted sesame seeds

*Glazed pecans may be found in the produce section of the supermarket with other salad toppings, or they may be found in the snack aisle. If unavailable, they can be prepared easily at home. (See Tip.)

**Crispy rice noodles may be found with canned chow mein noodles in the Asian section of the supermarket.

1 For dressing, whisk vinegar, garlic, sugar, salt and pepper in medium bowl until blended. Slowly whisk in olive oil and vegetable oil in thin, steady stream until well blended.

2 For salad, divide spinach among four serving bowls. Top with tomatoes, mandarin oranges, pecans, cheese, onion and cranberries. Sprinkle with rice noodles and sesame seeds. Drizzle 3 tablespoons dressing over each salad.

TIP

To make glazed pecans, combine 1 cup pecan halves, ¼ cup sugar, 1 tablespoon butter and ½ teaspoon salt in medium skillet; cook and stir over medium heat 5 minutes or until sugar mixture is dark brown and nuts are well coated. Spread on large plate; cool completely. Break into pieces or coarsely chop.

TACO SALAD SUPREME
MAKES 4 SERVINGS

CHILI

- 1 pound ground beef
- 1 medium onion, chopped
- 1 stalk celery, chopped
- 2 medium fresh tomatoes, chopped
- 1 jalapeño pepper, finely chopped
- 1½ teaspoons chili powder
- 1 teaspoon salt
- 1 teaspoon ground cumin
- ½ teaspoon black pepper
- 1 can (15 ounces) tomato sauce
- 1 can (about 15 ounces) kidney beans, rinsed and drained
- 1 can (about 15 ounces) pinto beans, rinsed and drained
- 1 cup water

SALAD

- 8 cups chopped romaine lettuce (large pieces)
- 2 cups diced fresh tomatoes
- 48 small round tortilla chips
- 1 cup salsa
- ½ cup sour cream
- ½ cup (2 ounces) shredded Cheddar cheese

1 For chili, combine beef, onion and celery in large saucepan; cook over medium-high heat 6 to 8 minutes or until beef is no longer pink, stirring to break up meat. Drain fat.

2 Add chopped tomatoes, jalapeño, chili powder, salt, cumin and black pepper; cook and stir 1 minute. Stir in tomato sauce, beans and water; bring to a boil. Reduce heat to medium-low; cook 1 hour or until most of liquid is absorbed.

3 For each salad, combine 2 cups lettuce and ½ cup diced tomatoes in individual serving bowl. Top with 12 tortilla chips, ¾ cup chili, ¼ cup salsa and 2 tablespoons sour cream. Sprinkle with 2 tablespoons cheese. (Reserve remaining chili for another use.)

HOUSE SALAD

MAKES 4 SERVINGS

DRESSING

- ½ cup mayonnaise
- ½ cup white wine vinegar
- ¼ cup grated Parmesan cheese
- 1 tablespoon olive oil
- 1 tablespoon lemon juice
- 1 tablespoon corn syrup
- 1 clove garlic, minced
- ¾ teaspoon Italian seasoning
- ½ teaspoon salt
- ½ teaspoon black pepper

SALAD

- 1 package (10 ounces) Italian salad blend
- 2 plum tomatoes, thinly sliced
- 1 cup croutons
- ½ cup thinly sliced red or green bell pepper
- ½ cup thinly sliced red onion
- ¼ cup sliced black olives
- Pepperoncini peppers (optional)

1 For dressing, whisk mayonnaise, vinegar, cheese, oil, lemon juice, corn syrup, garlic, Italian seasoning, salt and black pepper in medium bowl until well blended.

2 For salad, place salad blend in large bowl; top with tomatoes, croutons, bell pepper, onion, olives and pepperoncini, if desired. Add dressing; toss to coat.

WEDGE SALAD
MAKES 4 SERVINGS

DRESSING
- ¾ cup mayonnaise
- ½ cup buttermilk
- 1 cup crumbled blue cheese, divided
- 1 clove garlic, minced
- ½ teaspoon sugar
- ⅛ teaspoon onion powder
- ⅛ teaspoon salt
- ⅛ teaspoon black pepper

SALAD
- 1 head iceberg lettuce
- 1 large tomato, diced (about 1 cup)
- ½ small red onion, cut into thin rings
- ½ cup crumbled crisp-cooked bacon (6 to 8 slices)

1 For dressing, combine mayonnaise, buttermilk, ½ cup cheese, garlic, sugar, onion powder, salt and pepper in food processor or blender; process until smooth.

2 For salad, cut lettuce into quarters through stem end; remove stem from each wedge.

3 Place lettuce wedges on individual serving plates; top with dressing. Sprinkle with tomato, onion, remaining ½ cup cheese and bacon.

SANDWICHES

INSPIRED BY CORNER BAKERY®

TOMATO MOZZARELLA SANDWICH
MAKES 4 SERVINGS

BALSAMIC VINAIGRETTE

- 6 tablespoons extra virgin olive oil
- 3 tablespoons balsamic vinegar
- 1 clove garlic, minced
- 1 teaspoon honey
- 1 teaspoon Dijon mustard
- ½ teaspoon dried oregano
- ½ teaspoon salt
- ⅛ teaspoon black pepper

SANDWICHES

- 1 baguette, ends trimmed, cut into 4 equal pieces (4 ounces each) and split
- 1 cup loosely packed baby arugula
- 3 medium tomatoes, sliced ¼ inch thick
- 1 cup roasted red peppers, patted dry and thinly sliced
- 12 slices fresh mozzarella (one 8-ounce package)
- 12 fresh basil leaves

1 For vinaigrette, whisk oil, vinegar, garlic, honey, mustard, oregano, salt and black pepper in small bowl until well blended.

2 For each sandwich, drizzle 1 tablespoon vinaigrette over bottom half of bread. Layer with arugula, tomatoes, roasted peppers, cheese, additional arugula and basil. Drizzle with 1 tablespoon vinaigrette; replace top half of bread.

CLASSIC PATTY MELTS
MAKES 4 SERVINGS

5 tablespoons butter, divided

2 large yellow onions, thinly sliced

¾ teaspoon plus pinch salt, divided

1 pound ground chuck (80% lean)

½ teaspoon garlic powder

½ teaspoon onion powder

¼ teaspoon black pepper

8 slices marble rye bread

½ cup Thousand Island dressing

8 slices (about 1 ounce each) deli American or Swiss cheese

1 Melt 2 tablespoons butter in large skillet over medium heat. Add onions and pinch of salt; cook 20 minutes or until onions are very soft and golden brown, stirring occasionally. Remove to small bowl; wipe out skillet with paper towel.

2 Combine beef, remaining ¾ teaspoon salt, garlic powder, onion powder and pepper in medium bowl; mix gently. Shape into four patties about the size and shape of bread slices and ¼ to ½ inch thick.

3 Melt 1 tablespoon butter in same skillet over medium-high heat. Add patties, two at a time; cook 3 minutes or until bottoms are browned, pressing down gently with spatula to form crust. Turn patties; cook 3 minutes or until browned. Remove patties to plate; wipe out skillet with paper towel.

4 Spread one side of each bread slice with dressing. Top four bread slices with cheese slice, patty, caramelized onions, another cheese slice and remaining bread slices.

5 Melt 1 tablespoon butter in same skillet over medium heat. Add two sandwiches to skillet; cook 4 minutes or until golden brown, pressing down with spatula to crisp bread. Turn sandwiches; cook 4 minutes or until golden brown and cheese is melted. Repeat with remaining 1 tablespoon butter and sandwiches.

SPICY CHICKEN SANDWICH
MAKES 4 SERVINGS

2 boneless skinless chicken breasts (about 8 ounces each)

1½ cups buttermilk

3 tablespoons hot pepper sauce, divided

1 teaspoon salt

⅓ cup mayonnaise

1 teaspoon Cajun seasoning

Canola or vegetable oil for frying

1 cup all-purpose flour

½ cup cornstarch

2 teaspoons paprika

1½ teaspoons black pepper

1 teaspoon msg

1 teaspoon ground red pepper

4 brioche sandwich buns, toasted and buttered

12 to 16 dill pickle slices

1 Pound chicken to ½-inch thickness between two sheets of waxed paper or plastic wrap with rolling pin or meat mallet. Cut each breast in half crosswise to create total of four pieces. Cut off pointed ends, if necessary, for more even rectangular shapes.

2 Combine buttermilk, 2 tablespoons hot pepper sauce and salt in medium bowl; mix well. Add chicken to brine; cover and refrigerate at least 4 hours or overnight. Combine mayonnaise, remaining 1 tablespoon hot pepper sauce and Cajun seasoning in small bowl; cover and refrigerate until ready to serve.

3 Remove chicken from refrigerator about 30 minutes before cooking. Heat at least 3 inches of oil in large saucepan over medium-high heat to 350°F; adjust heat to maintain temperature. Meanwhile, combine flour, cornstarch, paprika, black pepper, msg and red pepper in shallow dish; mix well. Drizzle 4 tablespoons buttermilk brine into flour mixture; stir with fork or fingers until mixture resembles wet sand.

4 Working with one piece at a time, remove chicken from brine and add to flour mixture. Turn to coat completely, pressing flour mixture into chicken to form thick coating. Lower chicken gently into hot oil; fry 6 to 8 minutes or until cooked through (165°F) and crust is golden brown and crisp, turning occasionally. Drain on paper towel-lined plate.

5 Spread about 1½ tablespoons mayonnaise mixture on cut sides of buns. Top bottom halves of buns with three to four pickle slices, chicken and top halves of buns. Serve immediately.

NEW ORLEANS-STYLE MUFFALETTA

MAKES 4 TO 6 SERVINGS

¾ cup pitted green olives

½ cup pitted kalamata olives

½ cup giardiniera (Italian-style pickled vegetables), drained

2 tablespoons fresh parsley leaves

2 tablespoons capers

1 clove garlic, minced

2 tablespoons olive oil

1 tablespoon red wine vinegar

1 (8-inch) round Italian loaf (16 to 22 ounces)

8 ounces thinly sliced ham

8 ounces thinly sliced Genoa salami

6 ounces thinly sliced provolone cheese

1 Combine olives, giardiniera, parsley, capers and garlic in food processor; pulse until coarsely chopped and no large pieces remain. Transfer to medium bowl; stir in oil and vinegar until well blended. Cover and refrigerate several hours or overnight to blend flavors.

2 Cut bread in half crosswise. Spread two thirds of olive salad over bottom half of bread; layer with ham, salami and cheese. Spread remaining olive salad over cheese; top with top half of bread, pressing down slightly to compress. Wrap sandwich with plastic wrap; let stand 1 hour to blend flavors.

3 To serve sandwich warm, preheat oven to 350°F. Remove plastic wrap; wrap sandwich loosely in foil. Bake 5 to 10 minutes or just until sandwich is slightly warm and cheese begins to melt. Cut into wedges.

CHICKEN FAJITA ROLL-UPS

MAKES 4 SERVINGS

1 cup ranch dressing

1 teaspoon chili powder

2 tablespoons vegetable oil, divided

2 teaspoons lime juice

2 teaspoons fajita seasoning mix

½ teaspoon chipotle chili powder

¼ teaspoon salt

4 boneless skinless chicken breasts (about 6 ounces each)

4 fajita-size flour tortillas (8 to 9 inches)

1 cup (4 ounces) shredded Cheddar cheese

1 cup (4 ounces) shredded Monterey Jack cheese

3 cups shredded lettuce

1 cup pico de gallo

1 Combine ranch dressing and chili powder in small bowl; mix well. Refrigerate until ready to serve.

2 Combine 1 tablespoon oil, lime juice, fajita seasoning mix, chipotle chili powder and salt in small bowl; mix well. Coat both sides of chicken with spice mixture.

3 Heat remaining 1 tablespoon oil in large nonstick skillet or grill pan over medium-high heat. Add chicken; cook 6 minutes per side or until cooked through (165°F). Remove to plate; let stand 5 minutes before slicing. Cut chicken breasts in half lengthwise, then cut crosswise into ½-inch strips.

4 Wipe out skillet with paper towel. Place one tortilla in skillet; sprinkle with ¼ cup Cheddar and ¼ cup Monterey Jack. Heat over medium heat until cheeses are melted. Remove tortilla to clean work surface or cutting board.

5 Sprinkle ¾ cup shredded lettuce down center of tortilla; top with ¼ cup pico de gallo and one fourth of chicken. Fold bottom of tortilla up over filling, then fold in sides and roll up. Cut in half diagonally. Repeat with remaining tortillas, cheese and fillings. Serve with ranch dipping sauce.

CHEESY MUSHROOM MELT
MAKES 4 SERVINGS

4 French rolls
4 slices Swiss cheese
4 slices Cheddar cheese
4 slices provolone cheese
2 cups sliced mushrooms
1 avocado, thinly sliced
1 cup thinly sliced iceberg
    lettuce

½ cup thinly sliced yellow
    or white onion
2 plum tomatoes, thinly sliced
2 dill pickles, thinly sliced
    lengthwise
Optional toppings:
    mayonnaise, mustard,
    vinaigrette, sliced banana
    peppers and/or giardiniera

1 Preheat oven to 400°F. Line baking sheet with foil.

2 Split sides and long ends of rolls, leaving one long end attached. Place rolls cut sides down on prepared baking sheet. Bake 5 minutes.

3 Remove baking sheet from oven; turn rolls over. For each sandwich, cut one slice of each cheese in half diagonally; arrange cheese halves on each half of roll, overlapping to fit. Top each bottom half of roll with ½ cup mushrooms.

4 Bake 5 to 7 minutes or until cheese is melted and bread is toasted.

5 Layer avocado, lettuce, onion, tomatoes, pickles and desired toppings over mushrooms. Close sandwiches and press gently; cut in half to serve.

INSPIRED BY PANERA BREAD®

ALMOND CHICKEN SALAD SANDWICH

MAKES 4 SERVINGS

¼ cup mayonnaise

¼ cup plain Greek yogurt
  or sour cream

2 tablespoons cider vinegar

1 tablespoon honey

1 teaspoon salt

½ teaspoon black pepper

⅛ teaspoon garlic powder

2 cups chopped cooked chicken

¾ cup halved red grapes

1 large stalk celery, chopped

⅓ cup sliced almonds

  Leaf lettuce

1 tomato, thinly sliced

8 slices sesame semolina or
  country Italian bread

1 Whisk mayonnaise, yogurt, vinegar, honey, salt, pepper and garlic powder in small bowl until well blended.

2 Combine chicken, grapes and celery in medium bowl. Add dressing; toss gently to coat. Cover and refrigerate several hours or overnight. Stir in almonds just before making sandwiches.

3 Place lettuce and tomato slices on four bread slices; top with chicken salad and remaining bread slices. Serve immediately.

DOUBLE DECKER TACOS
MAKES 8 TACOS

2 tablespoons all-purpose flour
2 teaspoons chili powder
1 teaspoon dried minced onion
¾ teaspoon paprika
½ teaspoon salt
½ teaspoon garlic powder
¼ teaspoon sugar
1 pound ground beef
⅔ cup water

8 hard taco shells
8 mini (5-inch) flour tortillas*
2 cups refried beans, warmed
1 cup shredded romaine lettuce
1 cup chopped tomato
1 cup (4 ounces) shredded
   Cheddar cheese
Sour cream (optional)

*Mini flour tortillas may also
be labeled as street tacos.

1 Preheat oven to 350°F. Combine flour, chili powder, onion, paprika, salt, garlic powder and sugar in small bowl; mix well.

2 Cook beef in large skillet over medium-high heat 6 to 8 minutes or until browned, stirring to break up meat. Drain fat.

3 Add flour mixture; cook and stir 2 minutes. Stir in water; bring to a simmer. Reduce heat to medium; cook 10 minutes or until most of liquid has evaporated. Meanwhile, heat taco shells in oven 5 minutes or until warm.

4 Wrap tortillas in damp paper towel; microwave on HIGH 25 to 35 seconds or until warm. Spread each tortilla with ¼ cup refried beans, leaving ¼-inch border around edge. Wrap flour tortillas around outside of taco shells, pressing gently to seal together.

5 Fill taco shells with beef mixture; top with lettuce, tomato and cheese. Drizzle with sour cream, if desired. Serve immediately.

INSPIRED BY EINSTEIN BROS.® BAGELS

PEPPERONI PIZZA BAGELS

MAKES 4 SERVINGS

4 plain or sesame seed bagels
½ cup marinara sauce
1 cup (4 ounces) shredded
    mozzarella cheese

¼ cup mini pepperoni slices
Dried oregano (optional)

1 Preheat oven to 400°F. Line baking sheet with parchment paper or foil.

2 Cut bagels in half crosswise. Spread 1 tablespoon marinara sauce over each cut half; top with cheese and pepperoni. Place on prepared baking sheet.

3 Bake 8 to 10 minutes or until cheese is melted and beginning to brown. Sprinkle with oregano, if desired.

SANDWICHES

TUNA SALAD SANDWICH

MAKES 2 SERVINGS

1 can (12 ounces) solid white albacore tuna, drained

1 can (5 ounces) chunk white albacore tuna, drained

¼ cup mayonnaise

1 tablespoon pickle relish

2 teaspoons spicy brown mustard

1 teaspoon lemon juice

½ teaspoon salt

¼ teaspoon black pepper

2 pieces focaccia (about 4×3 inches), split and toasted *or* 4 slices honey wheat bread

Lettuce, tomato and red onion slices

1 Place tuna in medium bowl; flake with fork. Add mayonnaise, pickle relish, mustard, lemon juice, salt and pepper; mix well.

2 Serve tuna salad on focaccia with lettuce, tomato and onion.

THE GREAT REUBEN SANDWICH

MAKES 2 SANDWICHES

4 slices rye bread

¼ cup Thousand Island dressing (see Tip)

8 ounces thinly sliced corned beef or pastrami

4 slices (1 ounce each) Swiss cheese

½ cup sauerkraut, well drained

2 tablespoons butter

1 Spread one side of each bread slice with dressing. Top two bread slices with corned beef, cheese, sauerkraut and remaining bread slices.

2 Melt butter in large skillet over medium heat. Add sandwiches; press down with spatula or weigh down with small plate. Cook sandwiches 6 minutes per side or until cheese is melted and bread is lightly browned, pressing down with spatula to crisp bread slightly. Serve immediately.

TIP

For a quick homemade Thousand Island dressing, combine 2 tablespoons mayonnaise, 2 tablespoons sweet pickle relish and 1 tablespoon cocktail sauce.

MAIN DISHES

INSPIRED BY COOPER'S HAWK® WINERY & RESTAURANTS

SOY GINGER SALMON
MAKES 2 SERVINGS

¼ cup reduced-sodium soy sauce

2 tablespoons packed brown sugar

1 tablespoon grated fresh ginger

1 tablespoon butter

1 teaspoon Dijon mustard

2 teaspoons olive oil

2 salmon fillets (about 6 ounces each, 1 to 1¼ inches thick)

⅛ teaspoon black pepper

1 Preheat oven to 350°F. Combine soy sauce, brown sugar and ginger in small saucepan; bring to a simmer over medium heat. Cook 5 minutes or until slightly reduced and thickened. Remove from heat. Add butter and mustard; stir until butter is melted and mixture is smooth.

2 Heat oil in large nonstick ovenproof skillet over medium-high heat. Season salmon with pepper; add to skillet skin side up. Cook 2 to 3 minutes or until golden brown. Remove from heat; turn salmon and brush with soy sauce mixture.

3 Bake 6 to 8 minutes or until fish begins to flake when tested with fork, brushing with soy sauce mixture halfway through cooking. Brush with remaining mixture before serving.

ZUCCHINI NOODLES WITH ROASTED GARLIC CREAM SAUCE

MAKES 2 MAIN-DISH OR 4 SIDE-DISH SERVINGS

- 1 head garlic
- 2 tablespoons plus 1 teaspoon olive oil, divided
- 8 ounces sliced mushrooms
- 1 medium zucchini, cut into ½-inch pieces
- 1¼ teaspoons salt, divided
- ½ teaspoon black pepper, divided
- 1 pound zucchini noodles
- 2 tablespoons butter
- 1 small onion, finely chopped
- ¼ cup dry white wine
- ⅓ cup whipping cream
- ¼ cup milk
- 1 tablespoon water
- 1 teaspoon cornstarch
- 1 cup (4 ounces) shredded white Cheddar cheese, plus additional for garnish
- ¼ cup grated Parmesan cheese
- 2 cups packed fresh spinach, stemmed

1 To roast garlic, preheat oven to 400°F. Cut off ½ inch from top of garlic head to expose cloves. Place on small sheet of foil; drizzle with 1 teaspoon oil. Wrap garlic with foil to enclose. Roast about 45 minutes or until soft. Squeeze out roasted garlic from six cloves; chop or mash into paste. (Reserve remaining cloves for other recipes or spreading on bread.)

2 Add mushrooms to large saucepan or Dutch oven; cook over medium-high heat about 8 minutes or until mushrooms release liquid and begin to brown, stirring occasionally. Add 1 tablespoon oil, chopped zucchini, ½ teaspoon salt and ¼ teaspoon pepper; cook 5 minutes or until zucchini is crisp-tender, stirring occasionally. Transfer vegetables to large bowl; cover to keep warm.

3 Add remaining 1 tablespoon oil, zucchini noodles and ¼ teaspoon salt to same saucepan; cook over medium-high heat 2 to 3 minutes or until noodles are slightly softened, stirring with tongs. Add to bowl with vegetables.

4 Melt butter in same saucepan over medium heat. Add onion; cook and stir 3 minutes or until translucent. Add mashed roasted garlic; cook and stir 1 minute. Add wine; cook and stir 3 minutes or until almost evaporated. Stir in cream, milk, remaining ½ teaspoon salt and ¼ teaspoon pepper; bring to a simmer. Reduce heat to low; simmer 8 minutes, stirring occasionally.

5 Stir water into cornstarch in small bowl until smooth. Add to cream sauce over medium heat; cook and stir 1 minute or until thickened. Add 1 cup

Cheddar and Parmesan by handfuls, stirring until blended before adding more cheese.

6 Add spinach and mushroom-zucchini mixture to saucepan; toss gently to wilt spinach and coat vegetables with sauce. Add additional salt and pepper to taste. Serve immediately with additional Cheddar, if desired.

HARISSA HONEY CHICKEN

MAKES 4 SERVINGS

4 tablespoons olive oil, divided

3 tablespoons harissa

2 tablespoons honey, divided

2 tablespoons lemon juice

3 cloves garlic, minced

1½ teaspoons smoked paprika

1 teaspoon salt

1 teaspoon ground coriander

½ teaspoon ground cumin

1½ pounds boneless skinless chicken thighs (4 to 6)

Hot cooked rice (optional)

Optional toppings: shredded red cabbage, chopped cucumber, halved grape tomatoes, sliced green onion, crumbled feta cheese

1 Combine 2 tablespoons oil, harissa, 1 tablespoon honey, lemon juice, garlic, smoked paprika, salt, coriander and cumin in small bowl; mix well.

2 Place chicken in large resealable food storage bag. Pour harissa mixture over chicken; seal bag and massage marinade into chicken. Marinate in refrigerator at least 1 hour or up to 8 hours.

3 Remove chicken from refrigerator 30 minutes before cooking. Heat remaining 2 tablespoons oil in large skillet over medium-high heat. Add chicken in single layer; cook about 8 minutes or until browned. Turn and cook 8 minutes or until cooked through (165°F). Brush chicken with remaining 1 tablespoon honey, turning to coat both sides. Remove chicken to cutting board; let stand 5 minutes before chopping or slicing.

4 Chop chicken; serve with rice and desired toppings.

CAPELLINI PRIMAVERA

MAKES 6 SERVINGS

¼ cup (½ stick) butter

1 cup chopped onion

1 cup julienned or shredded carrots

4 cups (1-inch) broccoli florets (2 small heads)

1 package (8 ounces) sliced mushrooms

1 yellow squash, halved lengthwise and thinly sliced (about 2 cups)

2 teaspoons minced garlic

1 teaspoon salt

1 can (14 ounces) crushed tomatoes

½ cup drained oil-packed sun-dried tomatoes, finely chopped

1 tablespoon finely chopped fresh parsley

½ teaspoon dried oregano

½ teaspoon dried rosemary

⅛ teaspoon red pepper flakes

12 ounces uncooked angel hair pasta (capellini)

2 tablespoons olive oil

Black pepper

Grated Parmesan cheese (optional)

1 Melt butter in large skillet over medium-high heat. Add onion and carrots; cook and stir 3 minutes or until onion is softened. Add broccoli, mushrooms, squash, garlic and 1 teaspoon salt; cook 10 minutes or until mushrooms are tender, stirring frequently.

2 Reduce heat to medium-low. Add crushed tomatoes, sun-dried tomatoes, parsley, oregano, rosemary and red pepper flakes; cook 10 minutes, stirring occasionally.

3 Meanwhile, cook pasta in large saucepan of salted boiling water according to package directions for al dente. Drain and place in large serving bowl, reserving ½ cup pasta cooking water.

4 Stir reserved pasta cooking water into sauce; add sauce to pasta and toss to coat. Drizzle with oil; stir gently to coat. Season with additional salt and black pepper; serve with cheese, if desired.

MEXICAN PIZZA
MAKES 4 SERVINGS

1 pound ground beef

¾ cup water

1 package (about 1 ounce) taco seasoning mix

1 to 2 tablespoons vegetable oil

8 (8-inch) flour tortillas

1 can (15 ounces) refried beans

1 cup taco sauce, divided

1⅓ cups shredded Colby Jack or Mexican blend cheese

Optional toppings: diced fresh tomato, sliced black olives, sliced green onions, shredded lettuce

1 Preheat oven to 400°F. Line baking sheet with parchment paper.

2 Cook beef in medium skillet over medium-high heat about 6 to 8 minutes or until browned, stirring to break up meat. Drain fat. Stir in water and taco seasoning. Reduce heat to medium-low; cook about 10 minutes or until most of liquid is absorbed, stirring occasionally.

3 Meanwhile, heat 1 tablespoon oil in large skillet over medium-high heat. Cook tortillas in batches about 2 minutes per side or until crisp and lightly browned, adding additional oil as necessary. Drain on paper towel-lined plate. Arrange four tortillas on prepared baking sheet.

4 Heat refried beans in microwave or on stovetop according to package directions. Spread one fourth of beans (heaping ⅓ cup) over each tortilla on baking sheet. Top with one fourth of beef mixture (scant ½ cup); drizzle with 1 tablespoon taco sauce. Place remaining tortillas over beef mixture. Spread 3 tablespoons taco sauce over each tortilla; sprinkle with ⅓ cup cheese.

5 Bake 4 to 5 minutes or until cheese is melted. Immediately sprinkle with desired toppings. Cut into quarters.

MUSHROOM NOODLE STIR-FRY

MAKES 2 MAIN-DISH OR 4 SIDE-DISH SERVINGS

8 ounces uncooked Chinese egg noodles or spaghetti

8 ounces shiitake mushrooms, stemmed and thinly sliced (¼-inch slices)

Pinch of salt

2 tablespoons butter

1 tablespoon minced garlic

2 teaspoons honey

½ cup stir-fry sauce

2 to 3 tablespoons water

2 green onions, sliced diagonally

2 tablespoons grated Parmesan cheese

1 Cook noodles according to package directions; drain and rinse under cold water to stop cooking.

2 Heat large skillet over medium-high heat. Add mushrooms; cook and stir about 5 minutes or until browned. Season with salt. Add butter, garlic and honey; cook and stir 1 minute or until butter is melted and garlic is fragrant but not browned.

3 Add stir-fry sauce, 2 tablespoons water and noodles; cook and stir 2 to 3 minutes or until heated through. Add additional water by teaspoonful, if necessary, to loosen sauce.

4 Divide noodles between serving bowls; top with green onions and cheese.

BARBECUE CHICKEN PIZZA

MAKES 4 SERVINGS

1 tablespoon olive oil

6 ounces boneless skinless chicken breasts, cut into strips (about 2×¼ inch)

¼ teaspoon salt

⅛ teaspoon black pepper

6 tablespoons barbecue sauce, divided

1 package (16 ounces) refrigerated pizza dough, at room temperature

⅔ cup shredded mozzarella cheese, divided

½ cup shredded smoked Gouda cheese, divided

½ small red onion, cut vertically into ⅛-inch slices

2 tablespoons chopped fresh cilantro

1 Preheat oven to 450°F. Line baking sheet with parchment paper.

2 Heat oil in large skillet over medium-high heat. Season chicken with salt and pepper; cook 5 minutes or just until cooked though, stirring occasionally. Remove chicken to medium bowl. Add 2 tablespoons barbecue sauce; stir to coat.

3 Roll out dough into 12-inch circle on lightly floured surface. Transfer to prepared baking sheet. Spread remaining 4 tablespoons barbecue sauce over dough, leaving ½-inch border. Sprinkle with 2 tablespoons mozzarella and 2 tablespoons Gouda. Top with chicken and onion; sprinkle with remaining cheeses.

4 Bake 12 to 15 minutes or until crust is browned and cheese is bubbly. Sprinkle with cilantro.

BALSAMIC TOMATO PENNE
MAKES 4 TO 6 SERVINGS

1 package (16 ounces)
   uncooked penne pasta

6 tablespoons olive oil, divided

½ red onion, cut into
   ⅛-inch slices (1 cup)

¼ cup balsamic vinegar

4 plum tomatoes, cut into
   ½-inch pieces (2½ cups)

6 cloves roasted garlic*

1 teaspoon salt

1 package (5 ounces) fresh
   spinach, stemmed

Shredded Parmesan cheese

To roast garlic, cut top off one head of garlic to expose tops of cloves. Place on piece of foil; drizzle with 1 teaspoon olive oil and season lightly with salt. Wrap tightly in foil. Roast in preheated 400°F oven 35 to 45 minutes or until soft. Squeeze garlic from skins when cool enough to handle.

1 Cook pasta in large saucepan of salted boiling water according to package directions for al dente. Drain and place in large serving bowl; stir in 2 tablespoons oil.

2 Meanwhile, heat remaining ¼ cup oil in large skillet over medium-high heat. Add onion; cook and stir 5 minutes or until softened. Reduce heat to medium. Add vinegar; cook 3 minutes or until slightly reduced.

3 Add tomatoes, roasted garlic and salt; cook and stir 1 minute. Add spinach; cook 1 minute or just until wilted. Pour sauce over pasta; toss to coat. Serve with cheese.

CHEESY CHICKEN BAKE

MAKES 4 SERVINGS

1 package (16 ounces) refrigerated or thawed frozen pizza dough, at room temperature

½ cup plus 4 teaspoons Caesar salad dressing, divided

2 cups chopped cooked chicken

1 cup crumbled cooked bacon

1¼ cups (5 ounces) shredded Italian blend or mozzarella cheese, divided

1 Preheat oven to 425°F. Line baking sheet with parchment paper.

2 Divide dough into four pieces. Roll out each piece into 7½×5-inch rectangle on lightly floured surface.

3 Brush each piece of dough with 2 tablespoons dressing, leaving ¼-inch border. Top with ½ cup chicken, ¼ cup bacon and ¼ cup cheese. Starting with long side, roll up jelly-roll style; pinch seams to seal.

4 Place rolls seam side down on prepared baking sheet. Brush each roll with 1 teaspoon of remaining dressing; sprinkle with 1 tablespoon cheese.

5 Bake about 20 minutes or until golden brown. Serve warm.

SPICY PEANUT NOODLES

MAKES 2 TO 4 SERVINGS

1 package (about 14 ounces) Asian stir-fry wheat noodles (hokkien, udon or chow mein)

2½ tablespoons creamy peanut butter

3 tablespoons water, plus additional as needed

3 tablespoons soy sauce

2 tablespoons unseasoned rice vinegar

1 tablespoon packed brown sugar

1 tablespoon minced fresh cilantro

1 tablespoon chili oil

¼ teaspoon red pepper flakes

½ cucumber, peeled and julienned

Fresh cilantro leaves

1 Cook noodles according to package directions; drain.

2 Meanwhile, whisk peanut butter, 3 tablespoons water, soy sauce, vinegar, brown sugar, minced cilantro, chili oil and red pepper flakes in large bowl until smooth and well blended.

3 Add noodles; stir until well coated, adding additional water as needed to thin sauce. Cover and refrigerate until cold.

4 Divide noodles among four serving bowls; top with cucumber and cilantro.

NOTE

You can substitute 1 package (16 ounces) uncooked spaghetti or linguine for the Asian stir-fry noodles. Cook the pasta in a large saucepan of salted boiling water according to package directions for al dente. Drain and place in a large serving bowl, reserving some of the pasta cooking water to use in the sauce.

PARMESAN-CRUSTED CHICKEN

MAKES 4 SERVINGS

4 boneless skinless chicken breasts (about 6 ounces each)

¾ cup Italian salad dressing

2 tablespoons vegetable oil

¾ cup grated Parmesan cheese

¾ cup finely chopped provolone cheese

⅓ cup ranch dressing

1 cup panko bread crumbs

¼ cup (½ stick) butter, melted

1½ teaspoons garlic powder

1 Pound chicken to ¾-inch thickness between two sheets of waxed paper. Place chicken in large resealable food storage bag. Pour Italian dressing over chicken; seal bag and turn to coat. Marinate in refrigerator at least 30 minutes or overnight.

2 Preheat broiler. Line baking sheet or broiler pan with foil. Remove chicken from marinade; discard marinade. Heat oil in large skillet over medium-high heat. Add chicken; cook 5 to 6 minutes per side or until golden brown and cooked through.

3 Meanwhile, combine Parmesan, provolone and ranch dressing in medium bowl; mix well. Combine panko, melted butter and garlic powder in small bowl; mix well.

4 Transfer chicken to prepared baking sheet. Spread Parmesan mixture evenly over chicken; top with panko mixture.

5 Broil 3 to 4 minutes or until topping is golden brown.

MAIN DISHES

RESTAURANT-STYLE BABY BACK RIBS
MAKES 4 SERVINGS

1¼ cups water

1 cup white vinegar

⅔ cup packed dark brown sugar

½ cup tomato paste

1 tablespoon yellow mustard

1½ teaspoons salt

1 teaspoon liquid smoke

1 teaspoon onion powder

½ teaspoon garlic powder

½ teaspoon paprika

2 racks pork baby back ribs (3½ to 4 pounds total)

1 Combine water, vinegar, brown sugar, tomato paste, mustard, salt, liquid smoke, onion powder, garlic powder and paprika in medium saucepan; bring to a boil over medium heat. Reduce heat to medium-low; cook 40 minutes or until sauce thickens, stirring occasionally.

2 Preheat oven to 300°F. Place each rack of ribs on large sheet of heavy-duty foil. Brush some of sauce over ribs, covering completely. Fold down edges of foil tightly to seal and create packet; arrange packets on baking sheet, seam sides up.

3 Bake 2 hours. Prepare grill or preheat broiler. Carefully open packets and drain off excess liquid.

4 Brush ribs with sauce; grill or broil 5 minutes per side or until beginning to char, brushing with sauce once or twice during grilling. Serve with remaining sauce.

KUNG PAO SPAGHETTI

MAKES 4 TO 6 SERVINGS

½ cup reduced-sodium soy sauce

¼ cup dry sherry

4 tablespoons water, divided

3 tablespoons sugar

2 tablespoons chili garlic sauce

2 tablespoons red wine vinegar

1 tablespoon toasted sesame oil

3 tablespoons cornstarch, divided

1 package (16 ounces) uncooked spaghetti

1 pound boneless skinless chicken breasts, cut into 2- to 3-inch pieces

¼ teaspoon black pepper

2 tablespoons vegetable oil, divided

1 tablespoon minced garlic

½ cup dry roasted peanuts, coarsely chopped

1 bunch green onions (about 6), thickly sliced

1 For sauce, whisk soy sauce, sherry, 2 tablespoons water, sugar, chili garlic sauce, vinegar and sesame oil in small bowl until well blended. Stir remaining 2 tablespoons water into 2 tablespoons cornstarch in another small bowl until smooth.

2 Cook pasta in large saucepan of boiling salted water according to package directions for al dente. Drain and place in serving bowl; cover to keep warm.

3 Meanwhile, combine chicken, remaining 1 tablespoon cornstarch and pepper in medium bowl; toss until well coated. Heat 1 tablespoon vegetable oil in large skillet over medium-high heat. Add chicken; cook 5 to 7 minutes or until chicken is browned and cooked through, turning once. Stir in 2 tablespoons sauce; cook and stir 1 minute or until chicken is coated. Transfer chicken to plate; wipe out skillet with paper towel.

4 Heat remaining 1 tablespoon vegetable oil in same skillet over medium heat. Add garlic and peanuts; cook and stir 30 seconds or until garlic is fragrant but not browned. Add remaining sauce; heat to a simmer. Stir cornstarch mixture; add to sauce. Cook and stir 1 to 2 minutes or until sauce is thickened. Pour over pasta; toss to coat. Stir in peanuts and green onions. Divide spaghetti among serving bowls; top with chicken.

CHICKEN FRIED STEAK

MAKES 4 SERVINGS

STEAK

- ¾ cup all-purpose flour
- ½ teaspoon salt
- ½ teaspoon garlic powder
- ¼ teaspoon paprika
- ¼ teaspoon ground red pepper
- ¼ teaspoon black pepper
- ⅓ cup milk
- 1 egg
  Vegetable oil for frying
- 4 cube steaks (5 to 6 ounces each)

GRAVY

- ¼ cup all-purpose flour
- ½ teaspoon salt
- ¼ teaspoon black pepper
- 1½ cups milk
- ½ cup chicken broth
  Mashed potatoes (optional)
  Chopped fresh parsley (optional)

1 For steak, combine ¾ cup flour, ½ teaspoon salt, garlic powder, paprika, red pepper and ¼ teaspoon black pepper in shallow dish. Whisk ⅓ cup milk and egg in another shallow dish.

2 Heat about ¼ inch oil in large skillet over medium heat to 350°F. Pat steaks dry; coat both sides with flour mixture. Dip in egg mixture, letting excess drip back into dish, then coat again with flour mixture.

3 Cook steaks 4 to 6 minutes per side or until golden brown and crisp. Drain on paper towel-lined plate; transfer to wire rack to prevent coating from getting soggy. Tent with foil to keep warm.

4 For gravy, drain all but 3 tablespoons oil from skillet. Stir in ¼ cup flour, ½ teaspoon salt and ¼ teaspoon black pepper until well blended and smooth. Cook and stir over medium heat 2 minutes. Slowly whisk in 1½ cups milk and broth; bring to a boil, stirring constantly. Cook and stir 2 minutes or until thickened. Serve steaks over mashed potatoes, if desired; top with gravy and garnish with parsley.

COCONUT SHRIMP

MAKES 4 SERVINGS

DIPPING SAUCE
- ½ cup orange marmalade
- ⅓ cup Thai chili sauce
- 1 teaspoon prepared horseradish
- ½ teaspoon salt

SHRIMP
- 1 cup flat beer
- 1 cup all-purpose flour
- 2 cups sweetened flaked coconut, divided
- 2 tablespoons sugar
- Vegetable oil for frying
- 16 to 20 large raw shrimp, peeled and deveined (with tails on), patted dry

1 For sauce, whisk marmalade, chili sauce, horseradish and salt in small bowl until well blended. Cover and refrigerate until ready to serve.

2 For shrimp, whisk beer, flour, ½ cup coconut and sugar in large bowl until well blended. Refrigerate batter until oil is hot. Place remaining 1½ cups coconut in medium bowl.

3 Heat 2 inches of oil in large saucepan over medium heat to 350°F; adjust heat to maintain temperature. Dip each shrimp in beer batter, then in coconut, turning to coat completely.

4 Fry shrimp, four at a time, 2 to 3 minutes or until golden brown, turning halfway through cooking. Drain on paper towel-lined plate. Serve immediately with dipping sauce.

JAPANESE PAN NOODLES

MAKES 2 TO 4 SERVINGS

⅓ cup soy sauce

⅓ cup packed brown sugar

1 tablespoon mirin

1 teaspoon chili garlic sauce

1 tablespoon vegetable or peanut oil

2 cups small broccoli florets (about 2 small crowns or 10 ounces)

2 cups sliced mushrooms

1 cup matchstick carrots (about 2 medium) or shredded carrots

1 tablespoon finely chopped fresh ginger

1 package (14 to 16 ounces) cooked udon noodles*

Black sesame seeds

Fresh cilantro sprigs (optional)

Or substitute 1 package (16 ounces) dried or fresh udon noodles; cook and drain according to package directions.

1 Combine soy sauce and brown sugar in small saucepan; bring to a boil over medium-high heat. Reduce heat to medium; cook about 10 minutes or until reduced and thickened slightly, stirring frequently. Remove from heat; stir in mirin and chili garlic sauce until well blended.

2 Heat oil in wok or large saucepan over high heat. Add broccoli and mushrooms; cook and stir about 5 minutes or until vegetables are crisp-tender. Add carrots and ginger; cook and stir 1 minute.

3 Add soy sauce mixture and noodles; cook 3 to 5 minutes or until noodles are heated through and most of sauce is absorbed, stirring frequently.

4 Sprinkle with sesame seeds; garnish with cilantro.

CHICKEN MARSALA

MAKES 4 SERVINGS

4 boneless skinless
 chicken breasts
 (6 to 8 ounces each)

½ cup all-purpose flour

1 teaspoon coarse salt

¼ teaspoon black pepper

2 tablespoons olive oil

3 tablespoons butter, divided

2 cups sliced mushrooms

1 shallot, minced
 (about 2 tablespoons)

1 clove garlic, minced

1 cup dry Marsala wine

½ cup chicken broth

 Finely chopped fresh parsley

1 Cut chicken breasts in half crosswise. Pound each piece to ¼-inch thickness between two sheets of plastic wrap with meat mallet or rolling pin.

2 Combine flour, salt and pepper in shallow dish; mix well. Coat both sides of chicken with flour mixture, shaking off excess.

3 Heat oil and 1 tablespoon butter in large skillet over medium-high heat. Add chicken in single layer; cook about 4 minutes per side or until golden brown. Remove to plate; tent with foil to keep warm.

4 Add 1 tablespoon butter, mushrooms and shallot to skillet; cook 10 minutes or until mushrooms are deep golden brown, stirring occasionally. Add garlic; cook and stir 1 minute. Stir in wine and broth; cook 2 minutes, scraping up browned bits from bottom of skillet. Stir in remaining 1 tablespoon butter until melted.

5 Return chicken to skillet; turn to coat with sauce. Cook 2 minutes or until heated through. Sprinkle with parsley.

SIDE DISHES

INSPIRED BY CRACKER BARREL® OLD COUNTRY STORE

HEARTY HASH BROWN CASSEROLE
MAKES ABOUT 16 SERVINGS

2 cups sour cream

2 cups (8 ounces) shredded Colby cheese, divided

1 can (10¾ ounces) cream of chicken soup

½ cup (1 stick) butter, melted

1 small onion, finely chopped

¾ teaspoon salt

½ teaspoon black pepper

1 package (30 ounces) frozen shredded hash brown potatoes, thawed

1 Preheat oven to 375°F. Spray 13×9-inch baking dish with nonstick cooking spray.

2 Combine sour cream, 1½ cups cheese, soup, butter, onion, salt and pepper in large bowl; mix well. Add potatoes; stir until well blended.

3 Spread potato mixture in prepared baking dish. (Do not pack down.) Sprinkle with remaining ½ cup cheese.

4 Bake 45 minutes or until cheese is melted and top of casserole is beginning to brown.

OVEN-ROASTED VEGETABLES

MAKES 4 SERVINGS

8 ounces cremini mushrooms, halved or quartered if large

8 ounces Brussels sprouts, trimmed and quartered

2 carrots, diced (½-inch pieces)

2 parsnips, diced

1 medium red onion, diced

1 medium zucchini, diced

1 red bell pepper, diced

2 tablespoons olive oil

1 teaspoon salt

¼ teaspoon black pepper

1 tablespoon butter, melted

1 green onion, finely chopped

1 tablespoon chopped fresh basil

1 clove garlic, minced

1 tablespoon balsamic glaze

1 tablespoon grated Parmesan cheese

1 Preheat oven to 450°F. Combine mushrooms, Brussels sprouts, carrots, parsnips, red onion, zucchini, and bell pepper in large bowl. Drizzle with oil; season with salt and pepper and toss to coat. Spread in single layer on baking sheet.

2 Roast 15 minutes. Stir vegetables; roast 5 to 10 minutes or until crisp-tender. *Turn oven to broil.*

3 Drizzle vegetables with butter. Sprinkle with green onion, basil and garlic; stir to coat. Spread vegetables in single layer.

4 Broil 3 to 5 minutes or until edges of vegetables begin to brown. Drizzle with balsamic glaze; sprinkle with cheese.

CORN BREAD MUFFINS
MAKES 9 MUFFINS

1¼ cups yellow cornmeal
1 cup all-purpose flour
¼ cup granulated sugar
1 tablespoon baking powder
1 teaspoon salt

¾ cup milk
1 egg
¼ cup (½ stick) plus 1 tablespoon butter, melted, divided
¼ cup plus 1 tablespoon honey, divided

1 Preheat oven to 400°F. Spray 9 standard (2½-inch) muffin cups with nonstick cooking spray or line with paper baking cups.

2 Combine cornmeal, flour, sugar, baking powder and salt in large bowl; mix well. Whisk milk, egg, ¼ cup melted butter and ¼ cup honey in medium bowl until well blended. Add to cornmeal mixture; stir just until combined.

3 Spoon batter evenly into prepared muffin cups. (Batter will almost entirely fill cups.)

4 Bake 13 to 15 minutes or until toothpick inserted into centers comes out clean. Meanwhile, stir remaining 1 tablespoon melted butter and 1 tablespoon honey in small bowl until smooth.

5 Brush honey butter over muffins immediately after removing from oven. Cool muffins in pan 5 minutes; remove to wire rack. Serve warm.

SIDE DISHES

POLENTA FRIES
MAKES ABOUT 4 SERVINGS

3 cups water
1 teaspoon salt
1 cup yellow cornmeal
   Vegetable oil for frying

2 tablespoons grated
   Parmesan cheese
Aioli or favorite dipping sauce
   (optional)

1 Bring water and salt to a boil in medium saucepan over high heat. Very slowly add cornmeal, whisking vigorously to avoid forming lumps. Reduce heat to medium-low; cook about 20 minutes or until polenta is thick and pulls away from side of pan, stirring frequently.

2 Spray 9-inch square baking pan with nonstick cooking spray or line with parchment paper. Pour warm polenta into prepared pan, spreading into even layer about ½ inch thick. (Use offset spatula or dampened hands to help spread polenta.) Cover and refrigerate at least 2 hours or overnight until cold and completely firm.

3 Heat ¼ inch of oil in large skillet over medium heat to 350°F. Meanwhile, invert polenta onto cutting board; pat dry with paper towels to remove any excess moisture or condensation. Cut polenta into sticks about 3 inches long and ½ inch wide.

4 Add polenta sticks to hot oil in batches; cook 3 to 5 minutes per side or until golden brown. (Cook in single layer; do not crowd in skillet. Cooking times may vary depending on moisture level in polenta.) Drain on paper towel-lined plate. Sprinkle with cheese; serve immediately with aioli, if desired.

TIPS

You can bake the polenta sticks in the oven instead of pan-frying them. Line a baking sheet with parchment paper; spray with nonstick cooking spray. Cut the polenta into sticks as directed; brush with 1 teaspoon olive oil before separating the sticks and spreading them on the baking sheet. Bake on the lower rack in a preheated 425°F oven for 20 minutes. Turn the oven to broil and move the polenta to the top oven rack. Broil about 5 minutes or until golden brown. Sprinkle with cheese.

You can also add herbs or spices to the polenta for additional flavor. Stir in ¼ to ½ teaspooon garlic powder, onion powder and/or smoked paprika after blending the cornmeal into the boiling water.

STEAKHOUSE CREAMED SPINACH
MAKES 4 SERVINGS

1 pound baby spinach
½ cup (1 stick) butter
2 tablespoons finely chopped onion
¼ cup all-purpose flour
2 cups whole milk

1 bay leaf
½ teaspoon salt
Pinch ground nutmeg
Pinch ground red pepper
Black pepper

1 Heat medium saucepan of water to a boil over high heat. Add spinach; cook 1 minute. Drain and remove to bowl of ice water to stop cooking. Squeeze spinach dry; coarsely chop. Wipe out saucepan with paper towel.

2 Melt butter in same saucepan over medium heat. Add onion; cook and stir 2 minutes or until softened. Add flour; cook and stir 2 to 3 minutes or until slightly golden.

3 Slowly add milk in thin, steady stream, whisking constantly until mixture boils and begins to thicken. Stir in bay leaf, ½ teaspoon salt, nutmeg and red pepper. Reduce heat to low; cook and stir 5 minutes. Remove and discard bay leaf.

4 Add spinach; cook 5 minutes, stirring frequently. Season with additional salt and black pepper.

BROWN BREAD
MAKES 2 LOAVES

1 package (¼ ounce)
   active dry yeast
1¼ cups warm water
   (105° to 110°F)
¼ cup packed brown sugar
¼ cup molasses
2 tablespoons vegetable oil

1½ tablespoons unsweetened
   cocoa powder
1¼ teaspoons salt
2 cups all-purpose flour
1½ cups whole wheat flour
2 teaspoons old-fashioned oats

1 Dissolve yeast in water in large bowl of stand mixer; let stand 5 minutes or until bubbly. Stir in brown sugar, molasses, oil, cocoa and salt until well blended. Add all-purpose flour and whole wheat flour; stir until rough dough forms.

2 Mix with dough hook at low speed 5 minutes (dough will be slightly sticky but should clean side of bowl). Shape dough into a ball. Place in large greased bowl; turn to grease top. Cover and let rise in warm place 1½ to 2 hours or until doubled in size.

3 Line baking sheet with parchment paper. Turn out dough onto very lightly floured surface; divide in half. Shape each half into 12×3-inch loaf; place loaves on prepared baking sheet.

4 Moisten top and sides of loaves with dampened hands; sprinkle 1 teaspoon oats over top and sides of each loaf, pressing lightly to adhere. Loosely cover loaves and let rise in warm place 1 hour or until very puffy and almost doubled in height.

5 Preheat oven to 350°F. Bake 25 minutes or until bottoms of loaves are lightly browned and instant-read thermometer inserted into center of loaves registers 190°F. Remove to wire racks to cool. Serve warm or cool completely.

SIDE DISHES

PARMESAN ALFREDO PASTA BAKE
MAKES 6 TO 8 SERVINGS

2 tablespoons plus ½ teaspoon salt, divided

1 package (16 ounces) uncooked fusilli pasta

6 tablespoons (¾ stick) butter

1 clove garlic

1 cup whipping cream

1 cup milk

2 cups shredded Parmesan cheese, divided

1 cup (4 ounces) shredded mozzarella cheese

4 ounces mozzarella cheese, cubed

1 cup panko bread crumbs

2 tablespoons butter, melted

¼ teaspoon Italian seasoning

1 Preheat oven to 400°F. Spray 3-quart baking dish with nonstick cooking spray.

2 Bring large saucepan of water to a boil; stir in 2 tablespoons salt. Add pasta; cook according to package directions until al dente. Drain pasta, reserving ½ cup cooking water. Return pasta to saucepan.

3 Meanwhile, melt 6 tablespoons butter in medium saucepan over medium heat. Add garlic and remaining ½ teaspoon salt. Stir in cream, milk and reserved ½ cup pasta water; bring to a simmer. Remove from heat; remove and discard garlic clove. Gradually stir in 1 cup Parmesan and shredded mozzarella until smooth and well blended. Pour over pasta; stir gently to coat. Pour into prepared baking dish; fold in cubed mozzarella.

4 Combine panko, remaining 1 cup Parmesan and 2 tablespoons melted butter in medium bowl; mix well. Spread evenly over pasta mixture; sprinkle with Italian seasoning.

5 Bake 15 minutes or until topping is golden brown and pasta is heated through.

LOADED BAKED POTATOES
MAKES 4 SERVINGS

4 medium baking potatoes, baked

1 cup (4 ounces) shredded Cheddar cheese

1 cup (4 ounces) shredded Monterey Jack cheese

8 slices bacon, crisp-cooked

½ cup sour cream

¼ cup (½ stick) butter, melted

2 tablespoons milk

1 teaspoon salt

¼ teaspoon black pepper

1 tablespoon vegetable oil

2 teaspoons coarse salt

1 green onion, thinly sliced (optional)

1 Preheat oven to 400°F. Prick potatoes all over with fork; place in small baking pan. Bake 1 hour or until potatoes are fork-tender. Let stand until cool enough to handle. *Reduce oven temperature to 350°F.*

2 Combine Cheddar and Monterey Jack in small bowl; reserve ¼ cup for garnish. Chop bacon; reserve ¼ cup for garnish.

3 Cut off thin slice from one long side of each potato. Scoop out centers of potatoes, leaving ¼-inch shell. Place flesh from 3 potatoes in medium bowl. (Reserve flesh from fourth potato for another use.) Add sour cream, butter, remaining 1¾ cups shredded cheese, bacon, milk, 1 teaspoon salt and pepper to bowl with potatoes; mash until well blended.

4 Turn potato shells over; brush bottoms and sides with oil. Sprinkle evenly with coarse salt. Turn right side up and return to baking pan. Fill shells with mashed potato mixture, mounding over tops of shells. Sprinkle with reserved cheese and bacon.

5 Bake 20 minutes or until filling is hot and cheese is melted. Garnish with green onion.

CHICKEN FRIED RICE
MAKES 4 SERVINGS

2 tablespoons vegetable oil, divided

12 ounces boneless skinless chicken breasts, cut into ½-inch cubes

Salt and black pepper

2 tablespoons butter

2 cloves garlic, minced

½ sweet onion, diced

1 medium carrot, diced

2 green onions, thinly sliced, plus additional for garnish

3 eggs

4 cups cooked rice*

3 tablespoons soy sauce

2 tablespoons sesame seeds

For rice, cook 1½ cups rice according to package directions without oil or butter. Spread hot rice on large rimmed baking sheet; cool to room temperature. Refrigerate several hours or overnight. Measure 4 cups for recipe.

1 Heat 1 tablespoon oil in large skillet over medium-high heat. Add chicken; season with salt and pepper. Cook and stir 5 to 6 minutes or until cooked through. Add butter and garlic; cook and stir 1 minute or until butter is melted. Remove to medium bowl.

2 Add sweet onion, carrot and two green onions to skillet; cook and stir over high heat 3 minutes or until vegetables are softened. Add to bowl with chicken.

3 Heat remaining 1 tablespoon oil in same skillet. Crack eggs into skillet; cook and stir 45 seconds or until eggs are scrambled but still moist.

4 Return chicken and vegetable mixture to skillet with rice, soy sauce and sesame seeds; cook and stir 2 minutes or until well blended and heated through. Season with additional salt and pepper; garnish with additional green onion.

ROSEMARY BREAD
MAKES 2 SMALL LOAVES

1 tablespoon sugar

1 package (¼ ounce) active dry yeast

1 cup warm water (110°F)

2 tablespoons finely chopped fresh rosemary, divided

2½ to 2¾ cups all-purpose flour, divided

2 tablespoons olive oil

1⅛ teaspoons salt, divided

2 tablespoons butter, melted, divided

⅛ teaspoon black pepper

1 Dissolve sugar and yeast in warm water in large bowl of stand mixer; let stand 5 minutes or until bubbly. Reserve 1 teaspoon rosemary for topping; set aside.

2 Add 2½ cups flour, oil, remaining rosemary and 1 teaspoon salt to yeast mixture; stir until blended. Mix with dough hook at medium speed 5 minutes. Add additional flour, 1 tablespoon at a time, if dough is too sticky or does not clean side of bowl. Shape dough into a ball. Place in large greased bowl; turn to grease top. Cover and let rise in warm place about 1 hour or until doubled in size.

3 Line baking sheet with parchment paper. Gently punch down dough; divide in half. Shape each half into a ball; place on prepared baking sheet.

4 Brush loaves with 1 tablespoon butter; sprinkle with reserved rosemary, remaining ⅛ teaspoon salt and pepper. Cover loosely with plastic wrap and let rise in warm place about 45 minutes or until almost doubled in size. Preheat oven to 400°F.

5 Bake loaves 20 minutes or until golden brown. Brush with remaining 1 tablespoon butter. (Brush lightly to avoid removing seasoning from tops of loaves.) Remove to wire rack to cool completely.

BRUSSELS SPROUTS WITH HONEY BUTTER

MAKES 4 SERVINGS

6 slices thick-cut bacon, cut into ½-inch pieces

1½ pounds Brussels sprouts (about 24 medium), halved

¼ teaspoon salt

¼ teaspoon black pepper

2 tablespoons butter, softened

2 tablespoons honey

1 Preheat oven to 375°F. Cook bacon in medium skillet until almost crisp. Drain on paper towel-lined plate; set aside. Reserve 1 tablespoon drippings.

2 Place Brussels sprouts on large baking sheet. Drizzle with reserved bacon drippings and sprinkle with ¼ teaspoon salt and ¼ teaspoon pepper; toss to coat. Arrange Brussels sprouts cut sides down in single layer on baking sheet.

3 Roast 30 minutes or until Brussels sprouts are browned, stirring once.

4 Combine butter and honey in medium bowl; mix well. Add roasted Brussels sprouts; stir until completely coated. Stir in bacon; season with additional salt and pepper.

DESSERTS

INSPIRED BY JET'S PIZZA®

CHOCOLATE CHIP BROWNIE
MAKES 8 TO 10 SERVINGS

¾ cup all-purpose flour

½ cup unsweetened Dutch process cocoa powder

½ teaspoon salt

½ teaspoon baking powder

¾ cup granulated sugar

½ cup packed brown sugar

½ cup (1 stick) butter, melted

2 eggs

½ teaspoon vanilla

1 cup dark chocolate chips

1 Preheat oven to 350°F. Spray 9-inch round cake pan with nonstick cooking spray. Line bottom with parchment paper; spray paper with cooking spray.

2 Combine flour, cocoa, salt and baking powder in medium bowl; mix well. Whisk granulated sugar, brown sugar and butter in large bowl until well blended. Add eggs, one at a time, whisking until well blended after each addition. Whisk in vanilla until blended. Add flour mixture; stir just until blended. Stir in chocolate chips. Pour batter into prepared pan.

3 Bake 22 to 27 minutes or until brownie is just set to the touch and toothpick inserted into center comes out with fudgy crumbs. Cool in pan on wire rack.

4 To remove from pan, loosen edge with small knife; invert onto wire rack and invert again onto serving plate. Cut into wedges.

STRAWBERRY CREAM SHORTCAKE
MAKES 6 SERVINGS

CAKE

- 1½ cups all-purpose flour
- 2 teaspoons baking powder
- ½ teaspoon salt
- ½ cup (1 stick) butter, softened
- 1 cup granulated sugar
- 1 teaspoon vanilla
- 2 eggs
- ½ cup plus 2 tablespoons buttermilk

FROSTING

- 1 package (8 ounces) cream cheese, softened
- ¾ cup powdered sugar
- Pinch of salt
- 1¼ cups whipping cream
- 1 teaspoon vanilla (optional)
- 1 cup strawberry fruit spread*

STRAWBERRIES

- 1 package (16 ounces) fresh strawberries, stemmed and cut into wedges
- ½ cup granulated sugar

Or purée 1 cup strawberry jam or preserves in food processor or blender until smooth.

1 For cake, preheat oven to 350°F. Grease and flour three 8-inch square baking pans. Line bottoms of pans with parchment paper; spray paper with nonstick cooking spray. Combine flour, baking powder and ½ teaspoon salt in small bowl; mix well.

2 Beat butter and 1 cup granulated sugar in large bowl with electric mixer at medium speed 3 to 5 minutes or until light and fluffy. Beat in vanilla; scrape side of bowl. Add eggs, one at a time, beating well after each addition. With mixer running at low speed, alternately add flour mixture and buttermilk in three additions, beginning and ending with flour mixture. Scrape side of bowl; beat 30 seconds or until well blended. Divide batter among prepared pans; spread evenly to completely cover bottoms of pans. (Batter layers will be very thin.)

3 Bake 16 to 18 minutes or until edges are very lightly browned and toothpick inserted into centers comes out clean. Cool in pans on wire rack 10 minutes. Remove from pans; cool layers completely on parchment paper on wire rack.

4 For frosting, whip cream cheese, powdered sugar and pinch of salt in large bowl with electric mixer fitted with whisk attachment at low speed 1 minute or until blended. Increase speed to medium; whip 3 to 5 minutes

or until light and fluffy. Scrape side of bowl and whip 1 minute. With mixer running at medium speed, very slowly drizzle in cream; whip until frosting is fluffy and holds stiff peaks. Stir in vanilla, if desired.

5 Peel off parchment from cake layers. Place one layer, top side down, on serving plate or cutting board. Top with ½ cup fruit spread, spreading to within ½ inch of edge. Spread ¾ cup frosting over fruit spread. Top with second cake layer, top side down; repeat layers of fruit spread and frosting. Top with remaining cake layer, top side up; spread with remaining frosting. Refrigerate at least 2 hours before serving. Meanwhile, combine strawberries and ½ cup granulated sugar in medium bowl; cover and refrigerate until ready to serve.

6 To serve, trim about ½ inch from each side of cake. Cut cake into six pieces; place on serving plates. Spoon strawberry mixture over and around cake.

CHOCOLATE OAT DREAM BARS

MAKES 9 TO 12 SERVINGS

2¼ cups all-purpose flour

1 cup plus 2 tablespoons packed brown sugar

1 cup plus 2 tablespoons old-fashioned oats

¾ teaspoon baking soda

½ teaspoon salt

1 cup plus 2 tablespoons (2¼ sticks) butter, melted

1 teaspoon vanilla

3 tablespoons caramel sauce

¾ cup semisweet chocolate chips

1 Preheat oven to 350°F. Spray 9-inch baking pan with nonstick cooking spray.

2 Combine flour, sugar, oats, baking soda and salt in large bowl; mix well. Add butter and vanilla; mix with hands or stir with spatula until mixture is well blended and clumpy.

3 Press 3 cups dough (loosely packed) into bottom of prepared pan. Cover and refrigerate remaining dough until ready to use. Bake crust 13 minutes.

4 Remove pan from oven. Drizzle with caramel sauce; sprinkle with chocolate chips. Drop chunks of reserved dough (1- to 2-inch pieces) evenly over chocolate chips.

5 Bake 15 minutes or until lightly browned. Cool completely in pan on wire rack before cutting into bars.

CARAMEL FUDGE CRUMBLE ICE CREAM CAKE

MAKES 12 TO 16 SERVINGS

9 cups French vanilla or vanilla bean ice cream, divided

65 chocolate sandwich cookies, divided

¾ cup hot fudge topping, divided, plus additional for serving

1 jar (about 14 ounces) caramel sauce

1 package (8 ounces) English toffee bits

3 tablespoons butter, melted

Whipped cream and maraschino cherries (optional)

1 Line bottom of 9-inch springform pan with foil. Place 3 cups ice cream in medium bowl; let stand at room temperature 15 minutes or until softened. Place 30 cookies in food processor; process until fine crumbs form. Transfer to another medium bowl; stir in 6 tablespoons hot fudge topping until blended.

2 Combine caramel sauce and toffee bits in small bowl; mix well.

3 Place 15 cookies in food processor; process until fine crumbs form. Add butter; process until well blended and crumbs are moistened. Press evenly onto bottom of prepared pan. Top with softened ice cream, spreading into even layer (see Tip). Spread half of caramel mixture evenly over ice cream to within 1 inch of edge. Top evenly with half of hot fudge-cookie crumb mixture.

4 Place pan in freezer for 15 minutes to allow ice cream to harden. Meanwhile, place 3 cups ice cream in medium bowl; let stand at room temperature 15 minutes or until softened.

5 Remove pan from freezer; spread softened ice cream over cookie layer. Top with remaining caramel mixture and sprinkle with remaining half of hot fudge-cookie crumb mixture. Place pan in freezer 15 minutes to allow ice cream to harden. Meanwhile, place remaining 3 cups ice cream in medium bowl; let stand at room temperature 15 minutes or until softened. Remove pan from freezer; spread softened ice cream over cookie layer.

6 Place remaining 20 cookies in food processor; pulse until large crumbs form. Add remaining 6 tablespoons hot fudge topping; pulse until blended, leaving some larger pieces of cookies remaining. Sprinkle mixture over top ice cream layer, pressing in lightly. Cover with plastic wrap; freeze cake 4 hours or overnight.

7 Remove pan from freezer. Run long thin spatula under hot water; run spatula around edge of pan to loosen. Remove side of pan. Cut into wedges. Serve with additional hot fudge topping, if desired; garnish with whipped cream and cherry.

TIP

To easily spread ice cream into an even layer, use a small offset spatula that has been warmed in hot water. Fill a tall glass or measuring cup with hot water and dip the spatula in hot water frequently while spreading the ice cream.

LEMON MERINGUE PIE

MAKES 8 SERVINGS

1 frozen deep-dish pie crust

1 cup plus 6 tablespoons sugar, divided

1 cup lemon juice (from about 5 lemons)

2 tablespoons grated lemon peel

6 egg yolks

1 tablespoon cornstarch

¼ teaspoon plus pinch of salt, divided

½ cup (1 stick) butter, cut into cubes

4 egg whites

½ teaspoon cream of tartar

1 Preheat oven to 400°. Prick holes in bottom of crust with fork. Bake 10 minutes or until lightly browned. Cool completely on wire rack. *Reduce oven temperature to 325°F.*

2 Whisk 1 cup sugar, lemon juice, lemon peel, egg yolks, cornstarch and ¼ teaspoon salt in medium saucepan until well blended. Add butter; cook over medium heat 6 to 8 minutes or until mixture is thick, whisking constantly. Strain through fine-mesh strainer into pie crust.

3 Beat egg whites and cream of tartar in large bowl with electric mixer at medium-high speed until frothy. Gradually add remaining 6 tablespoons sugar and pinch of salt; beat about 3 minutes or until stiff peaks form. Spread meringue over top of pie.

4 Bake 20 minutes or until meringue is golden brown. Cool completely on wire rack. Refrigerate until ready to serve.

CANNOLI CAKE
MAKES 16 SERVINGS

CAKE

2½ cups all-purpose flour
1 tablespoon baking powder
1 teaspoon baking soda
1 teaspoon salt
1¼ cups buttermilk
½ cup vegetable oil
1½ teaspoons vanilla
1½ cups granulated sugar
½ cup (1 stick) butter, softened
3 eggs

FROSTING

2 cups (16 ounces) mascarpone cheese
½ cup ricotta cheese
¼ cup (½ stick) butter, softened
Grated peel of 1 orange (about 2 teaspoons)
1 teaspoon vanilla
Pinch of salt
5 to 6 cups powdered sugar
1 cup mini chocolate chips
Mini cannoli (optional)

1 Preheat oven to 350°F. Grease and flour three 8-inch round cake pans.

2 For cake, combine flour, baking powder, baking soda and salt in medium bowl; mix well. Whisk buttermilk, oil and vanilla in measuring cup until blended. Beat granulated sugar and ½ cup butter in large bowl with electric mixer at medium speed about 5 minutes or until light and fluffy. Add eggs, one at a time, beating until blended after each addition. Alternately add flour mixture and buttermilk mixture in three additions; beat just until blended. Divide batter evenly among prepared pans.

3 Bake 25 to 30 minutes or until toothpick inserted into centers comes out clean. Cool in pans 10 minutes; remove to wire racks to cool completely.

4 For frosting, beat mascarpone, ricotta and ¼ cup butter in large bowl with electric mixer at medium speed until well blended and smooth. Beat in orange peel, vanilla and salt. Gradually add 5 cups powdered sugar; beat until well blended. Add additional powdered sugar, ¼ cup at a time, if necessary to reach spreading consistency.

5 Place one cake layer on serving plate. Spread with 1 cup frosting; sprinkle with 2 tablespoons chocolate chips. Top with second cake layer; spread with 1 cup frosting and sprinkle with 2 tablespoons chocolate chips. Top with remaining cake layer; spread remaining frosting over top and side of cake. Press remaining chocolate chips into side of cake. Refrigerate at least 6 hours or overnight. Garnish with mini cannoli just before serving.

INSPIRED BY APPLEBEE'S® GRILL + BAR

COOKIES AND CREAM SHAKE

MAKES 1 SERVING

5 chocolate sandwich cookies, divided

¼ cup whole milk

2 cups vanilla ice cream

Whipped cream or whipped topping

1 Coarsely chop four cookies. Chop remaining cookie into smaller pieces; set aside for garnish.

2 Pour milk into blender; add ice cream and blend just until smooth. Add coarsely chopped cookies; pulse until blended.

3 Top shake with whipped cream; sprinkle with reserved cookie pieces.

INSPIRED BY MCDONALD'S®

SHAMROCK SHAKE

MAKES 1 SERVING

2 cups low-fat French vanilla ice cream

½ cup milk, divided

⅛ teaspoon peppermint extract

10 drops green food coloring

Whipped cream and maraschino cherry (optional)

1 Combine ice cream, ¼ cup milk, peppermint extract and green food coloring in blender; blend until smooth.

2 Add additional ¼ cup milk if needed to reach desired consistency. Garnish with whipped cream and cherry.

DESSERTS

COOKIES AND CREAM SHAKE

FUDGY COLA CAKE
MAKES 24 SERVINGS

CAKE

- 2 cups granulated sugar
- 2 cups all-purpose flour
- 1 teaspoon baking soda
- ½ teaspoon salt
- ½ cup buttermilk
- 2 eggs
- 1 teaspoon vanilla extract
- 1 cup cola
- ½ cup (1 stick) butter
- ½ cup vegetable oil
- ¼ cup unsweetened Dutch process or regular cocoa powder

ICING

- ½ cup (1 stick) butter
- ½ cup cola
- ¼ cup unsweetened Dutch process or regular cocoa powder
- 4 cups powdered sugar, sifted

1 Preheat oven to 350°F. Spray 13×9-inch baking pan with nonstick cooking spray.

2 For cake, sift granulated sugar, flour, baking soda and salt into large bowl. Whisk buttermilk, eggs and vanilla in measuring cup until blended. (Mixture may look curdled.)

3 Combine 1 cup cola, ½ cup butter, oil and ¼ cup cocoa in medium saucepan; bring to a boil over medium heat, stirring frequently. Pour over flour mixture; stir until blended. Stir in buttermilk mixture until blended. Pour batter into prepared pan.

4 Bake 30 to 35 minutes or until toothpick inserted into center comes out clean. Meanwhile, prepare icing.

5 For icing, combine ½ cup butter, ½ cup cola and ¼ cup cocoa in medium saucepan; bring to a boil over medium heat, stirring frequently. Remove from heat; whisk in powdered sugar until well blended and smooth. Pour icing evenly over warm cake. Cool to room temperature in pan on wire rack.

RED VELVET COOKIES

MAKES ABOUT 15 COOKIES

1¼ cups plus 2 tablespoons all-purpose flour

2 tablespoons unsweetened cocoa powder

½ teaspoon baking soda

½ teaspoon salt

¼ teaspoon instant coffee granules or espresso powder

½ cup (1 stick) butter, melted

½ cup packed brown sugar

¼ cup granulated sugar

1 egg

1 teaspoon vanilla

1½ teaspoons red food coloring gel *or* 2 teaspoons liquid red food coloring

1 teaspoon white vinegar

1 cup white chocolate chips, divided

1 Preheat oven to 350°F. Line two cookie sheets with parchment paper.

2 Combine flour, cocoa, baking soda, salt and coffee powder in medium bowl; mix well. Whisk butter, brown sugar and granulated sugar in large bowl until well blended and smooth. Whisk in egg and vanilla until blended.

3 Add food coloring and vinegar; whisk until well blended. Add flour mixture; stir until blended. Stir in ¾ cup white chips.

4 Using scant 3 tablespoons dough per cookie, scoop dough into balls* (slightly larger than golf ball, balls should not be smooth). Place 2 inches apart on prepared cookie sheets; press additional white chips into top of each cookie.

5 Bake 8 minutes or until cookies are slightly puffy in center. Lift cookie sheets up several inches and let them drop down onto oven racks, deflating centers of cookies. Bake 3 to 5 minutes or until edges of cookies are set. Lift and drop cookie sheets again on countertop before removing to wire racks. Cool completely on cookie sheets.

Use plastic gloves when working with dough to avoid staining your hands.

CONFETTI BUNDT CAKE

MAKES 16 SERVINGS

3 cups all-purpose flour

1 teaspoon baking powder

½ teaspoon salt

½ cup buttermilk

⅓ cup vegetable oil

2 teaspoons vanilla extract

2 cups granulated sugar

1 cup (2 sticks) butter, softened

1 package (8 ounces) cream cheese, softened

5 eggs

½ cup rainbow sprinkles

Cream Cheese Frosting (recipe follows)

1 Preheat oven to 325°F. Grease and flour 12-cup (10-inch) bundt pan.

2 Combine flour, baking powder and salt in medium bowl; mix well. Whisk buttermilk, oil and vanilla in measuring cup until blended.

3 Beat granulated sugar, butter and cream cheese in large bowl with electric mixer at medium speed 5 minutes or until light and fluffy. Add eggs, one at a time, beating until blended and scraping down bowl after each addition. Alternately add flour mixture and buttermilk mixture in three additions; beat just until blended. Stir in sprinkles. Pour batter into prepared pan.

4 Bake 1 hour 10 minutes or until toothpick inserted near center comes out with a few moist crumbs. Cool cake in pan 15 minutes; invert onto wire rack to cool completely.

5 Prepare frosting; use pastry bag with ½-inch round tip to pipe frosting on cake.

CREAM CHEESE FROSTING

Beat 2 ounces softened cream cheese and ¼ cup (½ stick) softened butter in medium bowl with electric mixer at medium speed until smooth and creamy. Gradually add 2 cups powdered sugar, beating until blended after each addition. Beat in 1 tablespoon milk and ¼ teaspoon vanilla. Increase speed to medium-high; beat 2 minutes or until frosting is light and fluffy.

PUMPKIN CHEESECAKE
MAKES 12 SERVINGS

CRUST
- 18 graham crackers (2 sleeves)
- ¼ cup sugar
- ⅛ teaspoon salt
- ½ cup (1 stick) butter, melted

FILLING
- 1 can (15 ounces) pure pumpkin
- ¼ cup sour cream
- 2 teaspoons vanilla
- 2 teaspoons ground cinnamon
- 1 teaspoon ground ginger
- ¼ teaspoon salt
- ¼ teaspoon ground cloves
- 4 packages (8 ounces each) cream cheese, softened
- 1¾ cups sugar
- 5 eggs
- Whipped cream

1 Line bottom of 9-inch springform pan with parchment paper. Spray bottom and side of pan with nonstick cooking spray. Wrap outside of pan with heavy-duty foil.

2 For crust, place graham crackers in food processor; pulse until fine crumbs form. Add ¼ cup sugar and ⅛ teaspoon salt; pulse to blend. Add butter; pulse until crumbs are moistened and mixture is well blended. Press onto bottom and all the way up side of prepared pan in thin layer. Refrigerate at least 20 minutes. Preheat oven to 350°F.

3 Bake crust 12 minutes; cool on wire rack. Bring large pot of water to a boil.

4 For filling, whisk pumpkin, sour cream, vanilla, cinnamon, ginger, ¼ teaspoon salt and cloves in medium bowl until well blended. Beat cream cheese and 1¾ cups sugar in large bowl with electric mixer at medium speed until smooth and creamy. With mixer running, beat in eggs, one at a time, until blended. Scrape side of bowl. Add pumpkin mixture; beat at medium speed until well blended. Pour filling into crust.

5 Place springform pan in large roasting pan; place in oven. Carefully add boiling water to roasting pan to come about halfway up side of springform pan.

6 Bake 1 hour 15 minutes or until top is set and lightly browned but center jiggles slightly. Remove cheesecake from water; remove foil. Cool to room temperature on wire rack. Run small thin spatula around edge of pan to loosen crust. (Do not remove side of pan.) Cover with plastic wrap; refrigerate 8 hours or overnight. Garnish with whipped cream.

TIRAMISU

MAKES 9 SERVINGS

¾ cup sugar

4 egg yolks

1 cup plus 2 tablespoons whipping cream, divided

16 ounces mascarpone cheese

½ teaspoon vanilla

¾ cup cold strong brewed coffee

¼ cup coffee-flavored liqueur

24 to 28 ladyfingers

2 teaspoons unsweetened cocoa powder

1 Fill medium saucepan half full with water; bring to a boil over high heat. Reduce heat to low to maintain a simmer. Whisk sugar, egg yolks and 2 tablespoons cream in medium metal bowl until well blended. Place bowl over simmering water; cook 6 to 8 minutes or until thickened, whisking constantly. Remove from heat; cool slightly. Whisk in mascarpone and vanilla until well blended and smooth.

2 Pour remaining 1 cup cream into large bowl of stand mixer; beat at high speed until stiff peaks form. Gently fold whipped cream into mascarpone mixture until no streaks of white remain.

3 Combine coffee and liqueur in shallow bowl; mix well. Working with one ladyfinger at a time, dip cookies briefly into coffee mixture. Arrange in single layer in 9-inch square baking pan, trimming cookies to fit as necessary.

4 Spread thin layer of custard over ladyfingers, covering completely. Dip remaining ladyfingers in remaining coffee mixture; arrange in single layer over custard. Spread remaining custard over cookies.

5 Place cocoa in fine-mesh strainer; sprinkle over custard. Refrigerate 2 hours or overnight.

CHOCOLATE LAVA CAKES

MAKES 8 SERVINGS

¾ cup (1½ sticks) butter, plus additional for greasing

2 tablespoons granulated sugar

6 ounces semisweet chocolate

1½ cups powdered sugar, plus additional for garnish

4 eggs

6 tablespoons all-purpose flour

¼ teaspoon salt

1 teaspoon vanilla

1 Preheat oven to 425°F. Grease eight 4-ounce ramekins or custard cups with butter; coat with granulated sugar.

2 Combine chocolate and butter in medium microwavable bowl; microwave on HIGH 1½ minutes or until melted and smooth, stirring every 30 seconds. Whisk in 1½ cups powdered sugar until well blended.

3 Whisk in eggs, one at a time, until well blended. Add flour and salt; mix well. Stir in vanilla. Pour batter evenly into prepared ramekins.

4 Bake 9 to 10 minutes or until cakes spring back when lightly touched but centers are soft. Let stand 1 minute. Loosen sides of cakes with knife; invert onto serving plates and let stand 10 seconds before removing ramekins. Sprinkle with additional powdered sugar, if desired. Serve immediately.

RESTAURANT INDEX

RECIPE INDEX

TRADEMARKS

Applebee's is a registered trademark of Applebee's Restaurants LLC.

Au Bon Pain is a registered trademark of ABP Corporation.

Baker's Square is a registered trademark of BBQ Holdings, Inc.

Benihana is a registered trademark of Benihana National Corp.

Bob Evans Restaurant is a registered trademark of Bob Evans Restaurants, LLC.

Boston Market is a registered trademark of Boston Market Corporation.

California Pizza Kitchen is a registered trademark of California Pizza Kitchen.

Carrabba's Italian Grill is a registered trademark of Bloomin' Brands, Inc.

Cava is a registered trademark of CAVA Group, Inc.

The Cheesecake Factory is a registered trademark of TFC Co. LLC.

Chick-fil-A is a registered trademark of Chick-fil-A.

Chili's is a registered trademark of Brinker International.

Chipotle Mexican Grill is a registered trademark of Chipotle Mexican Grill.

Claim Jumper is a registered trademark of Landry's Restaurants Inc.

Cooper's Hawk Winery & Restaurant is a registered trademark of Cooper's Hawk Intermediate Holding, LLC.

Corner Bakery is a registered trademark of CBC Restaurant Corp.

Costco is a registered trademark of Costco Wholesale Corporation.

Cracker Barrel is a registered trademark of CBOCS Properties, Inc.

Domino's is a registered trademark of Domino's IP Holder LLC.

Dunkin' is a registered trademark of Inspire Brands, Inc.

Earls Kitchen + Bar is a registered trademark of Earls Restaurants Ltd.

Einstein Bros. Bagels is a registered trademark of Einstein Noah Restaurant Group, Inc.

Famous Dave's BBQ is a registered trademark of BBQ Holdings, Inc.

Fazoli's is a registered trademark of Fazoli's System Management, LLC.

First Watch, The Daytime Café is a registered trademark of First Watch Restaurants, Inc.

Fogo de Chão is a registered trademark of Fogo de Chão – US, Inc.

Hooters is a registered trademark of Hooters of America, LLC.

IHOP is a registered trademark of IHOP RESTAURANTS LLC.

Jason's Deli is a registered trademark of Deli Management, Inc.

Jet's Pizza is a registered trademark of Jet's® America, Inc.

Lone Star Steakhouse is a registered trademark of LSF5 CACTUS, LLC.

Longhorn Steakhouse is a registered trademark of RARE Hospitality Management LLC.

McDonald's is a registered trademark of McDonald's.

Miller's Ale House is a registered trademark of Miller's Ale House, Inc.

Noodles & Company is a registered trademark of Noodles & Company.

Nothing Bundt Cakes is a registered trademark of Nothing Bundt Cakes Franchising, LLC.

Olive Garden is a registered trademark of Darden Concepts, Inc.

Outback Steakhouse is a registered trademark of Bloomin' Brands, Inc.

Panera Bread is a registered trademark of Panera Bread.

P.F. Chang's is a registered trademark of P.F. Chang's.

Popeyes is a registered trademark of Popeyes Louisiana Kitchen, Inc.

Potbelly Sandwich Shop is a registered trademark of Potbelly Sandwich Works, LLC.

Red Robin is a registered trademark of Red Robin International.

Romano's Macaroni Grill is a registered trademark of RMG ACQUISITION COMPANY LLC.

Ruth's Chris is a registered trademark of Ruth's Hospitality Group.

Seasons 52 Fresh Grill is a registered trademark of Darden Concepts, Inc.

Starbucks is a registered trademark of Starbucks Coffee Company.

Taco Bell is a registered trademark of Taco Bell IP Holder, LLC.

TGI Fridays is a registered trademark of TGI Fridays, Inc.

Wendy's is a registered trademark of Quality Is Our Recipe, LLC

Wingstop is a registered trademark of Wingstop Restaurants, Inc.

Wow Bao is a registered trademark of Wow Bao, LLC.

Yard House is a registered trademark of Darden Concepts, Inc.

METRIC CONVERSION CHART

VOLUME MEASUREMENTS (dry)

1/8 teaspoon = 0.5 mL
1/4 teaspoon = 1 mL
1/2 teaspoon = 2 mL
3/4 teaspoon = 4 mL
1 teaspoon = 5 mL
1 tablespoon = 15 mL
2 tablespoons = 30 mL
1/4 cup = 60 mL
1/3 cup = 75 mL
1/2 cup = 125 mL
2/3 cup = 150 mL
3/4 cup = 175 mL
1 cup = 250 mL
2 cups = 1 pint = 500 mL
3 cups = 750 mL
4 cups = 1 quart = 1 L

VOLUME MEASUREMENTS (fluid)

1 fluid ounce (2 tablespoons) = 30 mL
4 fluid ounces (1/2 cup) = 125 mL
8 fluid ounces (1 cup) = 250 mL
12 fluid ounces (1 1/2 cups) = 375 mL
16 fluid ounces (2 cups) = 500 mL

WEIGHTS (mass)

1/2 ounce = 15 g
1 ounce = 30 g
3 ounces = 90 g
4 ounces = 120 g
8 ounces = 225 g
10 ounces = 285 g
12 ounces = 360 g
16 ounces = 1 pound = 450 g

DIMENSIONS

1/16 inch = 2 mm
1/8 inch = 3 mm
1/4 inch = 6 mm
1/2 inch = 1.5 cm
3/4 inch = 2 cm
1 inch = 2.5 cm

OVEN TEMPERATURES

250°F = 120°C
275°F = 140°C
300°F = 150°C
325°F = 160°C
350°F = 180°C
375°F = 190°C
400°F = 200°C
425°F = 220°C
450°F = 230°C

BAKING PAN SIZES

Utensil	Size in Inches/Quarts	Metric Volume	Size in Centimeters
Baking or Cake Pan (square or rectangular)	8×8×2	2 L	20×20×5
	9×9×2	2.5 L	23×23×5
	12×8×2	3 L	30×20×5
	13×9×2	3.5 L	33×23×5
Loaf Pan	8×4×3	1.5 L	20×10×7
	9×5×3	2 L	23×13×7
Round Layer Cake Pan	8×1½	1.2 L	20×4
	9×1½	1.5 L	23×4
Pie Plate	8×1¼	750 mL	20×3
	9×1¼	1 L	23×3
Baking Dish or Casserole	1 quart	1 L	—
	1½ quart	1.5 L	—
	2 quart	2 L	—